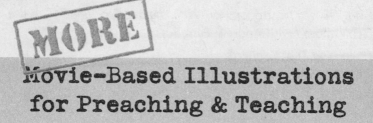

MORE

Movie-Based Illustrations
for Preaching & Teaching

Also by Craig Brian Larson

Movie-Based Illustrations for Preaching and Teaching
(coauthored with Andrew Zahn)

Preaching That Connects
(coauthored with Mark Galli)

MORE

Movie-Based Illustrations for Preaching & Teaching

101 Clips to Show or Tell

Craig Brian Larson & Lori Quicke

Editors of *Leadership* & PreachingToday.com

ZONDERVAN™

GRAND RAPIDS, MICHIGAN 49530 USA

More Movie-Based Illustrations for Preaching and Teaching
Copyright © 2004 by Christianity Today International

Requests for information should be addressed to:
Zondervan, *Grand Rapids, Michigan 49530*

ISBN 0-310-24834-5
Library of Congress Number 2002156682

Interior design by Todd Sprague

Printed in the United States of America

04 05 06 07 08 09 10 /❖ DC/ 10 9 8 7 6 5 4 3 2 1

Contents

Introduction

We are pleased to present *More Movie-Based Illustrations for Preaching and Teaching*. Movies have become the literature of our culture. Listen in on the conversations going on around you in a restaurant or at the mall, and you will hear people discussing the latest movies they've seen. Movies, therefore, are one bridge we can walk to connect with hearers where they are. Like literature, they offer a vast array of scenes, situations, and stirring stories (exactly what preachers crave)—things that preachers and teachers cannot always get just from their personal experience. Movies are a treasure-house of metaphors and phrases. Mention a movie in a sermon, and watch everyone turn a listening ear.

Aware of this, in early 2001 PreachingToday.com began including movie illustrations in our weekly batch of ten new illustrations. The companion volume *Movie-Based Illustrations for Preaching and Teaching* gathered together the first 101 movie illustrations in our database. This present volume now compiles our seventy-five newest movie illustrations and also adds twenty-six new movie illustrations that have never appeared on our site.

Each illustration includes relevant Scripture passages and multiple keywords that are thoroughly indexed. Each illustration gives a brief statement on the content rating of the movie. Even if you never go to the movies yourself, you have what you need to illustrate from them.

You do not have to show the movie clip in order to use these illustrations. We have written these in a way that assumes the movie clip will not be shown—providing necessary plot summary and describing the crucial scene concretely—but we have included elapsed times so that those who do show the clip can easily find the scene.

Avoiding the Objectionable

How do we decide which movies are worthy of drawing out illustrations? In this book we do not illustrate from any movie regarded as having no redeeming value. In addition, we do not illustrate with any scene that contains objectionable elements. In other words, we illustrate from some PG-13 or R rated movies, but we use no PG-13 or R rated scenes.

Thus the illustrations in this book do not use scenes that contain profanity, because we want preachers to be able to show the clips during the message if they choose. If some objectionable element in the movie immediately precedes or follows a selected clip, we include a warning.

How to Get Copyright Permission to Show Movie Clips

Do you need permission to show movies (even short clips) in church? *Yes* (although permission is not needed just to tell the illustration). You could argue the "fair use" copyright rule for using snippets of movies for sermon illustrations—that's what allows preachers to quote brief selections from books and articles—but the safer and more ethical approach is to purchase a license.

The licensing system works a lot like the CCLI license many churches purchase in order to be able to print or project song lyrics. In fact, Christian Copyright Licensing International (CCLI) has recently partnered with Motion Picture Licensing Corporation (MPLC) to offer a service especially for churches. Church Video Licensing International (CVLI) offers an "umbrella license" for an annual fee. You can show authorized titles from MPLC's long list of big studios (including Sony, Warner Brothers, and Disney) and from a growing list of Christian movie producers. This license covers clips in sermons, plus videos shown in classes and youth groups and at events such as family film nights—as long as no admission fee is charged and the title is not advertised to the general public.

Licensing fees are based on church size. An average Sunday attendance under five hundred is $180 a year; under a thousand is $240; up to fifteen hundred is $350; under two thousand is $475; three thousand and up is $600 a year. Smaller churches can license only the religious titles if they wish: $45 for churches with average attendance under a hundred, $75 for an average attendance under two hundred. Licenses can be granted over the phone, just in time for your next sizzling sermon illustration or Sunday night's Billy Graham film. Contact Christian Video Licensing International at 1-888-771-CVLI (2854)—on the Internet at http://www.cvli.org—or their sister organization, Motion Picture Licensing Corporation, 5455 Centinela Avenue, Los Angeles, CA 90066–6970. Contact them by e-mail at info@mplc.com or by telephone at 310-822-8855 or 1-800-462-8855 (visit them on the Internet at http://www.mplc.com).

Craig Brian Larson
Editor, PreachingToday.com

1. ACCEPTANCE

Forrest Gump

Topic: *Accepted with Flaws*

Texts: *John 13:20; Romans 5:8; Romans 15:7*

Keywords: *Acceptance; Brotherly Love; Caring; Christ's Love; Church; Community; Compassion; Gift of Salvation; God's Love; Human Help; Kindness; Mercy*

In *Forrest Gump,* the mentally challenged and physically disabled Forrest Gump (played by Tom Hanks) reminisces about the ups and downs of his unique life. Early in the movie, Forrest recalls his first day of school. He says, "You know it's funny how you remember some things, but some things you can't? I remember the bus ride on the first day of school very well."

The movie shifts back to Forrest's first day of school when, encumbered with bulky leg braces, he waddles toward the school bus. The bus door opens to reveal a scowling bus driver with a cigarette hanging from her mouth. Forrest pauses at the entrance to the bus and examines the bus driver with a look of uncertainty. The annoyed bus driver growls at Forrest, "Are you coming on?"

Forrest replies, "Mama said not to be taking rides from strangers."

Her patience waning, the bus driver gruffly responds, "This is the bus to school."

Forrest hits on a solution and says, "I'm Forrest, Forrest Gump."

The bus driver's countenance softens, and she introduces herself. "I'm Dorothy Harris."

Forrest says, "Well, now we ain't strangers anymore," and he boards the bus.

Unfortunately, the children on the bus are cold to Forrest. As Forrest begins the long trek down the bus's center aisle, he is shunned by his classmates: "Seat's taken." "Taken." "Can't sit here."

As the adult Forrest thinks back on that day, the pain on his face turns to wonder as he remembers how kindness and acceptance bubbled up amidst the rejection. "You know, it's funny what a young man recollects. 'Cause I don't remember bein' born. I don't recall what I got for my first Christmas, and I don't remember when I went on my first outdoor picnic. But I do remember when I heard the sweetest voice in the wide world."

Next to the cutest blonde-headed girl on the bus was an empty seat. "You can sit here if you want," she said.

Forrest muses, "I had never seen anything so beautiful in my life. She was like an angel."

Elapsed time: Measured from the beginning of the opening credit, this scene begins at 00:12:05 and ends at 00:13:58.

Content: Rated PG-13 for nudity, violence, and profanity

Citation: *Forrest Gump* (Paramount Pictures, 1994), written by Eric Roth, directed by Robert Zemeckis

submitted by David Slagle, Wilmore, Kentucky

2. ACCEPTANCE

The Joy Luck Club

Topic: *Mother Accepts Daughter*

Texts: *Romans 15:7; Colossians 3:21;
1 Thessalonians 5:11*

Keywords: *Acceptance; Anger; Bitterness; Blame;
Children; Conflict; Confrontation; Expectations; Failure;
Family; Humiliation; Mothers; Parenting; Rejection;
Resentment; Self-Pity; Self-Worth; Shame*

The Joy Luck Club, based on Amy Tan's novel, is about the strained relationships between four Chinese-born mothers and their adult American-born daughters. As the daughters mature, the mothers' expectations of how a woman should live conflict with the values and goals of their American daughters.

In one scene, June (played by Ming-Na Wen) and her mother clean up after a dinner party. The mother (played by Kieu Chinh) notices that June is upset. During the party, June felt slighted by her mother. Her mother asks, "So it's me you're mad at?"

Defensive, June responds, "I'm just sorry that you got stuck with such a loser, that I've always been so disappointing."

"What you mean 'disappoint'? Piano?"

June shakes her head and lists her failures: "Everything. My grades. My job. Not getting married. Everything you expected of me."

Her mother answers defensively, "Not expect anything! Never expect! Only hope! Only hoping best for you. That's not wrong, to hope."

June blurts out, "No? Well, it hurts, because every time you hoped for something I couldn't deliver, it hurt! It hurt me, Mommy. And no matter what you hope for, I'll never be more than what I am. And you never see that, what I really am!"

June's mother stares at her, tears welling up in her eyes. Then she takes the chain off her neck and offers it to June, who refuses it. Her mother says in a pleading tone, "June, since your baby time, I wear this next to my heart. Now you wear next to yours. It will help you know, I see you. I see you."

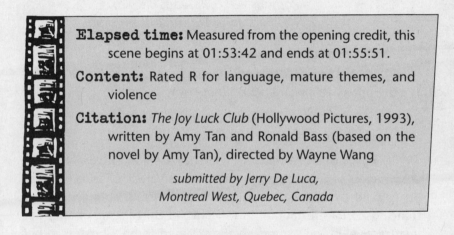

Elapsed time: Measured from the opening credit, this scene begins at 01:53:42 and ends at 01:55:51.

Content: Rated R for language, mature themes, and violence

Citation: *The Joy Luck Club* (Hollywood Pictures, 1993), written by Amy Tan and Ronald Bass (based on the novel by Amy Tan), directed by Wayne Wang

submitted by Jerry De Luca,
Montreal West, Quebec, Canada

3. ACCEPTANCE

My Big Fat Greek Wedding

Topic: *Unexpected Acceptance*

Texts: *Romans 12:13; Romans 14:1;*
Romans 15:7; Romans 16:16;
1 Corinthians 16:20; 2 Corinthians 13:12;
1 Peter 4:9

Keywords: *Acceptance; Church; Community; Culture;*
Family; Fellowship; Hospitality; Joy; Love

My Big Fat Greek Wedding is a comedy based on the real-life experiences of Greek-American actress Nia Vardalos. Toula Portokalos (played by Nia) is the daughter of a restaurateur who owns Dancing Zorba's restaurant in Chicago. At thirty years of age, this unattractive, portly woman seems doomed to be a hostess in her father's restaurant the rest of her life. But Toula has dreams of getting a college degree and falling in love.

Toula meets Ian Miller (played by John Corbett), a longhaired English teacher, and they immediately hit it off. As the relationship develops, Toula becomes increasingly concerned that, because Ian is not Greek, her parents (played by Michael Constantine and Lainie Kazan) will not approve of the relationship. But Toula persists in persuading her family that she has found the man of her dreams. Even though they gradually consent to their daughter's choice, the family insists that Ian adopt their Greek culture and faith.

When Ian's parents (a wealthy couple without any extended family) accept a dinner invitation at Toula's parents' home, they are not prepared for what they experience. As the Millers (played by Bruce Gray and Fiona Reid) drive into the suburban Chicago neighborhood, they can't help but notice that the Portokalos's garage door has been painted into a huge Greek flag. Even more amazing, they are greeted on the front lawn by nearly a hundred people—the entire Portokalos clan. Amid the dozens of cousins, aunts, and uncles (most of whom are named "Nick"), there is a goat hanging on a spit over an open fire.

Toula's father, Gus, addresses the Millers above the boisterous crowd. He smiles broadly and says, "Welcome to my home!" Toula's mother approaches the bewildered couple and gives them the traditional hug and kiss on the cheek. The deer-in-the-headlights expression on the faces of the Millers relaxes as they realize how much they are loved. Gus and his extended family then warmly welcome them inside the home for an evening of Greek-style feasting and hospitality.

Elapsed time: This scene begins at 01:05:00 and ends at approximately 01:06:40.

Content: Rated PG for sensuality and language

Citation: *My Big Fat Greek Wedding* (IFC Films, 2002), written by Nia Vardalos, directed by Joel Zwick

submitted by Greg Asimakoupoulos, Naperville, Illinois

17

4. ACCEPTANCE

Shrek

Topic: *Looking beyond Appearance*

Texts: *1 Samuel 16:7; Romans 15:7;
1 Corinthians 13; James 2:1–9;
1 John 4:18*

Keywords: *Acceptance; Appearance; Community;
Fear; Friendship; Judging Others; Loneliness; Love;
Relationships*

The animated movie *Shrek* celebrates the worth of society's under-valued people. It revolves around a boorish ogre, Shrek (voiced by Mike Myers), who finds a friend in a talking donkey (voiced by Eddie Murphy) and unexpectedly falls in love with a princess (voiced by Cameron Diaz), whom he rescues from a castle. This fairy-tale spoof emphasizes how humans place too much importance on outward appearance.

After freeing the princess, Shrek and Donkey escort her back to the village in keeping with the prince's orders. Because the journey is long, they decide to camp out. Around the campfire, Donkey talks to Shrek about what life will be like once they return to Shrek's home, a humble swamp.

Looking up at the sky, Donkey asks, "Hey Shrek, what are we going to do when we get back to our swamp anyway?"

"Our swamp?" Shrek challenges. "There's no *our*. There's just me and my swamp. And the first thing I'm gonna do is build a ten-foot wall around my land."

Donkey is surprised. He thought they had developed a friendship that would result in sharing their lives and possessions once the quest was over.

"You cut me deep, Shrek!" Donkey confesses. "You cut me real deep just now. Hey, you know what I think? I think this whole wall thing is just a way to keep somebody out."

The two argue and exchange verbal jabs. At last Donkey asks, "Who are you trying to keep out? Just tell me that, Shrek. Who?"

"Everyone! Okay?" Shrek exclaims.

"Hey, what's your problem, Shrek? What do you got against the whole world?"

The huge ogre seems almost childlike as he candidly explains, "Look, I'm not the one with the problem, okay? It's the world that seems to have a problem with me. People take one look at me and go 'Ahhh! Help! Run! It's a big, stupid, ugly ogre!' They judge me before they even know me. That's why I'm better off alone."

Donkey joins Shrek and says, "You know what? When we first met, I didn't think you were just a big, stupid, ugly ogre."

"Yeah, I know," Shrek acknowledges with gratitude. For the first time he realizes someone has looked beyond his outward appearance and accepted him—just as he is.

Elapsed time: Measured from the beginning of the opening credit, this scene begins at 00:45:50 and lasts approximately two minutes.

Content: Rated PG for vulgarity and scenes of violence

Citation: *Shrek* (DreamWorks, 2001), written by Ted Elliott and Terry Rossio, directed by Andrew Adamson and Vicky Jenson

submitted by Greg Asimakoupoulos, Naperville, Illinois

5. AFTERLIFE

Stepmom

Topic: *Longing for Life after Death*

Texts: *Romans 8:17–25; 1 Corinthians 15:13–23; 1 Thessalonians 4:13–18; 1 Peter 1:3–6*

Keywords: *Afterlife; Death; Heaven; Ideologies and Belief Systems; Illusions; Loss*

Stepmom is about the difficult and strained relationship between a new stepmother and her husband's ex-wife. Both must learn to deal with and accept one another in their new roles, especially as they both attempt to raise the ex-wife's two young children.

In one Christmas scene, eight-year-old Benjamin (played by Liam Aiken) enters the bedroom of his mother (played by Susan Sarandon), who is dying of cancer. He is excited as she gives him his Christmas present—a magician's cape with photographs of the two of them embedded on it. Benjamin sits in front of her and asks, "Are you dying?"

His mother pauses for a moment, then asks, "What do you think?"

Sadly he answers, "Yes. I won't see you anymore."

She tells him, "Well, you won't see my body, but—you know how a caterpillar becomes something else?"

Benjamin nods. "A butterfly."

She continues, "Yeah, you just have to think of me as off flying somewhere. And of course, a magician knows the secret that just because you don't see something, it doesn't mean it's not there." She makes a coin appear from his ear, and they both laugh.

Benjamin asks her where she'll be. She takes his hand, kisses it, places it in front of his heart, and says, "Right here. Inside the magician."

"Can I talk to you when you're there?"

"Always. Always. Always. You won't hear my voice, but, deep inside, you'll know what I'm saying."

"It's not good enough."

"No, no, of course it isn't, because it isn't everything. And we want everything, don't we? But we still have one thing. One of the greatest things we will always have. Do you know what that is? Our dreams." Benjamin smiles at this. "We can still meet in our dreams. We can talk to each other there, go for walks together in the summer and in the winter and in the rain and in the sun. I can come and pick you up and we can go flying."

Starting to get teary-eyed, he says, "Nobody loves you more than me."

He gives her a big hug as she says, "Nobody ever will."

Elapsed time: This scene begins at 01:51:00 and ends at 01:54:20.

Content: Rated PG-13 for language and thematic elements

Citation: *Stepmom* (Columbia TriStar, 1998), written by Gigi Levangie, directed by Chris Columbus

*submitted by Jerry De Luca,
Montreal West, Quebec, Canada*

6. ATTITUDE

How the Grinch Stole Christmas

Topic: *Changed Attitude*

Texts: *John 1:9; John 3:3; Acts 9:1–6; 1 Corinthians 6:6–11; 2 Corinthians 5:17; James 1:22*

Keywords: *Actions; Attitude; Change; Christmas; Conversion; Happiness; Joy; Materialism; New Birth; New Life; Redemption*

How the Grinch Stole Christmas is based on the classic holiday poem by Dr. Seuss. The Grinch, a hairy, green, cantankerous beast (played by Jim Carrey), looks down on the town of Whoville from his home on top of a mountain of garbage. What he sees disgusts him. The people who live in Whoville (called the Whos) love Christmas and all its trappings. Possessions, decorations, lights, and partying consume the Whos. The Grinch's disgust originated when he was mocked as a child because of his odd looks and the Christmas gift he made by hand. The Whos hate the Grinch as much as he loathes them.

Intent on destroying Christmas, the Grinch single-handedly devastates Whoville by stealing all their presents and Christmas trees. Tucked in his hideaway, he prepares to destroy all the loot he had stuffed into a gigantic pack. But before he can, he hears the townspeople singing in the valley.

The narrator (voiced by Anthony Hopkins) explains: "Then the Grinch heard a sound rising over the snow. It started in low. Then it started to grow." The Grinch grimaces as the narrator continues: "But the sound wasn't sad, but merry! VERY! Every Who down in Whoville, the tall and the small, was singing! Without any presents at all!"

The Grinch is bewildered by these people who are robbed of their possessions, yet are happy and singing.

So explains the narrator: "He HADN'T stopped Christmas from coming! IT CAME! Somehow or other, it came just the same. And the Grinch, with his grinch-feet ice-cold in the snow, stood puzzling and puzzling: How could it be so."

Finally the Grinch speaks: "It came without ribbons! It came without tags! It came without packages, boxes, or bags! Maybe Christmas doesn't come from a store. Maybe Christmas, perhaps, means a little bit more."

His eyes grow warm and soft and as big as saucers. Suddenly he throws himself to the ground, convulsing as his heart grows three times the size it was before. He laughs. He cries. He claims to feel all toasty inside. Unfamiliar with tears, he thinks he is leaking, while a brilliant shaft of sunlight bathes his green face and reveals a sincere smile. The conversion of the Grinch is matched by a brilliant sunrise.

But then it dawns on him that the stolen gifts are about to slide off the mountain and be destroyed. For the first time he actually cares. Transformed, he risks his life to keep the gifts from falling from the precipice. The Grinch's changed heart is matched by changed behavior.

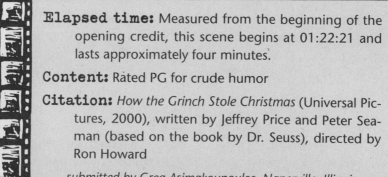

Elapsed time: Measured from the beginning of the opening credit, this scene begins at 01:22:21 and lasts approximately four minutes.

Content: Rated PG for crude humor

Citation: *How the Grinch Stole Christmas* (Universal Pictures, 2000), written by Jeffrey Price and Peter Seaman (based on the book by Dr. Seuss), directed by Ron Howard

submitted by Greg Asimakoupoulos, Naperville, Illinois

7. CHALLENGE

Music of the Heart

Topic: *Music Teacher Challenges Students*

Texts: *1 Corinthians 10:11; Ephesians 4:15; Ephesians 6:4; Colossians 3:16; 1 Thessalonians 5:12–14; 2 Thessalonians 3:14–15; 1 Timothy 5:20; Titus 2:15*

Keywords: *Accountability; Admonishment; Challenge; Correction; Criticism; Discipline; Exhortation; Leadership; Love; Mentoring; Rebuke; Teachability; Warnings; Youth*

Music of the Heart is based on the life of Roberta Guaspari (played by Meryl Streep), a single mother who teaches the violin in inner-city New York. Her passion and commitment inspire thousands of young people to excel in music and in life.

In one scene, Roberta meets with the school principal and a student's mother, who argues that Roberta shouts at her students. Roberta maintains she only does so when they don't listen. The mother asks, "Didn't you tell them that they were making their parents sick?"

Roberta laughs uncomfortably and tells her she didn't say exactly that.

The mother insists, "I'm raising Becky in a supportive atmosphere. I didn't send her to school to be abused."

Roberta responds, "I'm just trying to teach them discipline, that's all. If you want to take a very difficult instrument, you have to take it seriously. You have to focus. You have to pay attention."

The principal interrupts Roberta and tells her she should soften her comments. Roberta reluctantly agrees.

In the next scene, Roberta is instructing her students, who are all about ten years old. They are out of sync and playing badly, and they know it. Roberta pauses and says, "Well, that was pretty good. Not so bad."

The students are surprised, and one says, "It wasn't. We stunk."

Roberta responds, "Well, I wouldn't put it that way. I would just say that people could practice a little bit more." She asks a student if he practiced, and he says no. She encourages him to try a little harder for next week. "All you have to do is your best."

One of the students speaks up and asks, "Roberta, why are you acting like that, like, nice?"

"Well, don't you want a nice teacher?"

He answers that he already has nice teachers and wants variety.

Another student says, "We like you better the way you used to be." All the students agree.

One girl says, "I agree. This is even worse. You're acting weird now."

Roberta smiles and says, "Okay, I take it all back. You stunk!" All the kids laugh. "Don't tell your parents I said that. Let's do it again. Right this time. Stand up straight."

Elapsed time: Measured from the beginning of the opening credit, this scene begins at 00:38:58 and ends at 00:41:40.

Content: Rated PG for language and sensuality

Citation: *Music of the Heart* (Miramax Films, 1999), written by Pamela Gray (based on the book by Roberta Guaspari), directed by Wes Craven

submitted by Jerry De Luca,
Montreal West, Quebec, Canada

8. CHILDLIKENESS

Jack

Topic: *Childlike Adult Makes Friends*

Texts: *Matthew 6:25–34; Matthew 18:3–4; Matthew 19:14; Mark 10:13–16*

Keywords: *Anxiety; Attitudes and Emotions; Childlikeness; Fear; Joy; Worry*

The movie *Jack* is about a boy whose body ages at four times the normal rate. Although he thinks and feels like a ten-year-old, Jack (played by Robin Williams) has the body of a forty-year-old.

Jack's private tutor convinces the boy's parents to let Jack attend public school. At first, the schoolchildren snicker and joke about "the giant" with the hairy arms and a receding hairline. But in time, Jack's childlike joy captures the hearts of his schoolmates. One boy named Louis (played by Adam Zolotin) becomes Jack's best friend, and they share several boyhood adventures. Jack's influence soon begins to transform Louie's troubled, sometimes cynical, outlook on life.

Late in the movie, Jack's teacher (played by Jennifer Lopez) assigns Jack's class an essay: "What I Want to Be When I Grow Up." Louie's turn to read his paper falls on a day when Jack is late for school.

Standing in front of the class, reading from a piece of notebook paper, Louis says, "I want to be just like my best friend when I grow up. He's only ten, but he looks much older.

"He's like the perfect grown-up, because on the inside he's still just a kid. He's not afraid to learn things or try things, or to meet new people, the way most grown-ups are. It's like he's looking at everything for the first time, because he is. Most grown-ups aren't like that. Most grown-ups just want to go to work and make money and show up the neighbors.

"And more than anything, he knows how to be a great friend. More than most people who look like adults."

Just then, Jack enters the room. The students' faces light up with big smiles, and they give high fives as Jack walks by.

Louis continues, "So I may not know what I want to be when I grow up, and right now, I don't care. But I do know who I want to be like. I want to be like the giant, the big guy, my best friend, Jack."

Elapsed time: Measured from the beginning of the opening credit, this scene begins at 01:40:00 and ends at 01:41:57.

Content: Rated PG-13 for sexual references

Citation: *Jack* (Hollywood Pictures, 1996), written by James DeMonaco and Gary Nadeau, directed by Francis Ford Coppola

submitted by Drew Zahn, Stratford, Iowa.

9. CHILDREN OF GOD

The Princess Diaries

Topic: *Surprised to Learn We Are Royalty*

Texts: *Romans 8:15–17; Romans 8:28–30; 1 Corinthians 3:21–23; 2 Corinthians 6:18; Galatians 3:29; Ephesians 1:18; 1 Peter 2:9–10; Revelation 1:6; Revelation 5:10*

Keywords: *Children of God; Family of God; Fatherhood of God; Identity in Christ; Inheritance; Spiritual Adoption*

The Princess Diaries tells the story of Amelia (Mia) Thermopolis (played by Anne Hathaway), an average, awkward teenager whose estranged grandmother (played by Julie Andrews) comes to America to give Mia the biggest news of her life.

Mia visits her grandmother at her opulent mansion in San Francisco. A butler leads Mia to the grand living room, where she stands amazed as several servants bustle about. Suddenly all the servants stand at attention as Mia's grandmother enters the room. The contrast between Mia and her refined grandmother is painfully apparent. After some small talk, Mia, feeling uncomfortable, finally asks her grandmother, "What is it you want to tell me?"

Her grandmother answers, "Something, I believe, that will have a very big impact on your life." They walk outside to talk, and her grandmother begins to explain. "Amelia, have you ever heard of Eduard Cristof Philip Gerard Renaldi?"

"No," Mia responds. Her grandmother tells her he was the crown prince of Genovia.

Mia is as baffled as she is indifferent and shrugs her shoulders. "What about him?" she asks.

Her grandmother says, "Eduard Cristof Philip Gerard Renaldi was also your father."

Thinking her grandmother is only joking, she laughs, rolls her eyes in disbelief, and says, "If he was a prince, that would make me a . . ."

"Exactly," says her grandmother. "A princess. You see, you are not just Amelia Thermopolis. You are Amelia Mignonette Thermopolis Renaldi, the princess of Genovia."

Mia can hardly speak as this new revelation sinks in. "Me—a—a—a princess?"

The Bible says we are heirs of the God of the universe. The implications of that are far more surprising.

Elapsed time: Measured from the beginning of the opening credit, this scene begins at 00:12:28 and ends at 00:13:52.

Content: Rated G

Citation: *The Princess Diaries* (Walt Disney Pictures, 2001), written by Gina Wendkos (based on the novel by Meg Cabot), directed by Garry Marshall

submitted by David Slagle, Wilmore, Kentucky

10. CHOICES

Dangerous Minds

Topic: *Choosing Hope*

Texts: *Deuteronomy 30:15–20; Joshua 24:15; Psalm 119:30–32*

Keywords: *Admonishment; Choices; Correction; Cynicism; Despair; Disillusionment; Doubt; Education; Failure; Hope; Hopelessness; Leadership; Mentoring; Potential; Poverty; Rebuke; Responsibility; Servanthood; Teachers; Teaching; Teenagers; Youth*

Dangerous Minds is based on a true story about high school teacher LouAnne Johnson (played by Michelle Pfeiffer) making a difference in the lives of troubled but smart inner-city students.

In one scene, while LouAnne is in front of the class teaching, the students are upset with her because they felt she "ratted" on three students for fighting. LouAnne asks them if they want to discuss the issue. There is no response. Fully calm and composed, she tells them if they feel so strongly about it, they should leave the classroom. No one is forcing them. They can stay or leave.

One of the students objects and tells her they don't have a choice. "If we leave, we don't get to graduate. If we stay, we have to put up with you."

LouAnne tells the student that's a choice—not one they like, but it's a choice.

Another student angrily objects and says, "Man, you don't understand nothing. You don't come from where we live. You're not bused here. You come and live in my neighborhood for one week, and then you come and tell me if you have a choice."

LouAnne, with a slight tinge of anger, firmly replies, "There are a lot of people who live in your neighborhood who choose not to get on that bus. What do they choose to do? They choose to go out and sell drugs. They choose to go out and kill people. They choose to do a lot of other things. But they choose not to get on that bus. The people who choose to get on that bus, which are you, are the people who are saying, 'I will not carry myself down to die; when I go to my grave, my head will be high.' That is a choice." Then in a slightly louder and angrier tone, she says, "There are no victims in this classroom!"

The camera shows one student seriously considering her words.

Another female student says, "Why do you care anyway? You're just here for the money."

LouAnne quickly responds, "Because I make a choice to care, and honey, the money ain't that good."

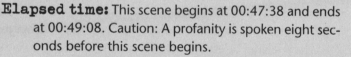

Elapsed time: This scene begins at 00:47:38 and ends at 00:49:08. Caution: A profanity is spoken eight seconds before this scene begins.

Content: Rated R for language

Citation: *Dangerous Minds* (Buena Vista, 1995), written by Ronald Bass (based on the book *My Posse Don't Do Homework* by LouAnne Johnson), directed by John N. Smith

submitted by Jerry De Luca,
Montreal West, Quebec, Canada

11. CHOICES

Kate and Leopold

Topic: *Choosing the Better Way*

Texts: *Deuteronomy 30:19; Psalm 63:3; Hosea 11:4; John 10:10*

Keywords: *Abundant Life; Choices; Christ's Love; Decisions; Divine Love; Eternal Life; God's Love; Love; Love for Christ; Romantic Love*

In *Kate and Leopold,* Kate McKay (played by Meg Ryan) is an advertising executive in New York City, bounding up the corporate ladder, yet bored with her career. Her friend Stuart surprises her with news he has found a breach in the fabric of time: by leaping off the Brooklyn Bridge at a calculated date, time, and height, he traveled back to the nineteenth century, and he returned with an aristocratic bachelor as proof.

When Kate meets Leopold, the Duke of Albany (played by Hugh Jackman), she is wowed by Leo's old-fashioned charm and grace. Not only does she hire him to do a margarine commercial set in the 1800s, but she also allows him to break into a previously guarded heart. Leo's integrity, chivalry, and honor mesmerize Kate. He is everything she has ever hoped for in a man.

Leopold declares his love for her, yet she hesitates, afraid to commit completely to him. Disappointed, Leo returns to the nineteenth century.

At the same time, Kate is promoted to president of her company. Although her new job comes with more money, more prestige, and the corner office, she realizes the life Leo offers outweighs all she previously thought was more important.

In a meeting, she stands before the corporate crowd and says, "It's a good thing to get what you want." Her boss looks on proudly. Out of the corner of her eye, she spies photographs of Leopold on the podium. She pauses awkwardly and then continues, "Unless what you thought you wanted wasn't really what you wanted, because what you really wanted you couldn't imagine or didn't think was possible." Her boss shifts in his seat as Kate fingers the photographs.

She continues, "What if someone came along who knew exactly what you wanted without asking? They just knew, like they could hear your heart beating or listen to your thoughts. And what if they were sure of themselves, and they didn't have to take a poll, and they loved you, and you hesitated?"

At once Kate realizes she must make a decision: will she embrace a lifestyle of success, power, and self-actualization, or will she respond to the love of a person who offered her a life unlike anything she thought possible? Even though it will mean turning her back on her promotion and taking a leap of faith by jumping off the Brooklyn Bridge to return to Leopold, she knows this is what she wants to do.

"I have to go," she says. Her colleagues don't know what she's alluding to, but she repeats herself with increased conviction, "I'm sorry, but I really have to go."

Kate then goes to the bridge and enters the time portal to be reunited with Leopold.

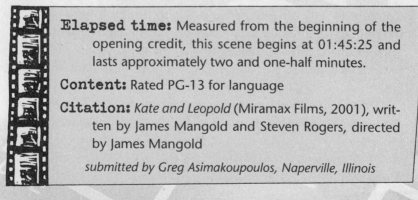

Elapsed time: Measured from the beginning of the opening credit, this scene begins at 01:45:25 and lasts approximately two and one-half minutes.

Content: Rated PG-13 for language

Citation: *Kate and Leopold* (Miramax Films, 2001), written by James Mangold and Steven Rogers, directed by James Mangold

submitted by Greg Asimakoupoulos, Naperville, Illinois

12. CHRIST'S AUTHORITY

Gladiator

Topic: *Power of Jesus' Name*

Texts: *Luke 10:17–19; John 18:3–6; Acts 2:31–36; Ephesians 1:19–22; Philippians 2:8–11; Colossians 2:9–15; Revelation 5; Revelation 6:17; Revelation 12:10; Revelation 19:11–18*

Keywords: *Afterlife; Authority; Christ's Authority; Divine Vengeance; God's Kingdom; Identity in Christ; Lordship of Christ; Names of Christ; Names of God; Power; Reputation*

Set in AD 180, *Gladiator* tells the story of General Maximus Decimus Meridius (played by Russell Crowe), who was about to be given reigning authority in Rome by the aging emperor, Marcus Aurelius. Before this could take place, however, the emperor's son, Commodus, killed his father in order to establish himself on the throne. He then ordered the murder of Maximus and his family. Maximus escaped, and the movie follows him as he is sold into slavery, becomes a nameless gladiator, and finally seeks justice against wicked Emperor Commodus.

The turning point comes late in the movie. After Maximus wins a great battle in the coliseum, Emperor Commodus decides to meet this unknown gladiator face-to-face. The crowd watches as the emperor in full pomp strides with his soldiers onto the sands of the coliseum.

The emperor asks the simple question: "What is your name?"

Maximus, streaked with blood and dirt from the battle, takes off his helmet and says, "My name is Maximus Decimus Meridius, commander of the armies of the north, general of the Felix legions, loyal servant to the true emperor, Marcus Aurelius, father to a murdered son, husband to a murdered wife. And I will have my vengeance, in this life or the next."

The crowd erupts with a deafening roar, while the emperor visibly shakes under the weight of the true identity of a man he thought was a mere slave. The emperor flees the coliseum, only to face defeat and death later at the hands of Maximus.

Elapsed time: This scene begins at 01:28:30 and ends at 01:32:00.

Content: Rated R for violence

Citation: *Gladiator* (DreamWorks, 2000), written by David Franzoni, directed by Ridley Scott

submitted by Bill White, Paramount, California

13. CHRIST AS SUBSTITUTE

The Green Mile

Topic: *Cost of Healing*

Texts: *Leviticus 16:10; Isaiah 53:4–5; Luke 8:43–48; 2 Corinthians 5:21; 1 Peter 2:24*

Keywords: *Atonement; Christ as Burden Bearer; Christ as Substitute; Christ's Cross; Healing; Humanity of Christ; Sacrifice; Sin*

The Green Mile is set in the south in 1935. Paul Edgecomb (played by Tom Hanks) is head guard of death row in a Louisiana prison. It is called "the green mile" because of the long, lime-colored floor prisoners walk to get to the electric chair.

John Coffey (played by Michael Clarke Duncan) is a slightly retarded, seven-foot black man who has been falsely charged with the murder of two little white girls.

Paul discovers John possesses a mysterious gift. He can absorb another's disease and cure them. When the prison warden's wife (played by Patricia Clarkson) is diagnosed with an inoperable brain tumor, Paul arranges for his guards to secretly transport John to the woman's home in the middle of the night. As the guards escort John into the house, the warden's wife is screaming like a possessed woman. John goes to her bedside and looks into a face contorted by pain. The woman suddenly relaxes and asks him his name.

John smiles, "John Coffey, ma'am. Like the drink, only not spelt the same."

He then leans over her face and says, "I see it!"

Sensing something mysterious going on, the woman begins to whimper, "What's happening to me?"

John says, "Shhh! You be still now. You be so quiet and so still!"

As the warden looks on, John places his mouth next to hers. The inside of her mouth begins to glow as a swarm of bugs streams out of her mouth into his. The room grows bright. The pendulum on the grandfather clock stops and the crystal shatters. The house rocks as if hit by an earthquake. As John sits up, the woman's face is peaceful and serene. The disease has left her body. But as John doubles over in pain and begins to cough uncontrollably, we realize he has taken her sickness to himself.

Elapsed time: Measured from the beginning of the opening credit, this scene begins at 02:14:22 and lasts about two and one-half minutes.

Content: Rated R for language, violence, and some sexual material

Citation: *The Green Mile* (Warner Brothers, 1999), written and directed by Frank Darabont (based on the novel by Stephen King)

submitted by Greg Asimakoupoulos, Naperville, Illinois

14. CHURCH AS FAMILY OF GOD

Ice Age

Topic: *Sacrificial Community*

Texts: *Acts 2:42–47; Romans 12:10; 1 Corinthians 12:14–27; Galatians 3:26–29; Galatians 6:1–2; Philippians 2:1–4; 1 Thessalonians 5:11–14; Hebrews 10:24–25; James 5:19–20; 1 Peter 1:22; 1 Peter 2:9–10; 1 Peter 2:17*

Keywords: *Caring; Church as Family of God; Church's Care; Community; Love; Ministry; Pastors; Sacrifice; Unity; Unity of the Church*

In the animated movie *Ice Age,* when saber-toothed tigers attack a tribe of nomads, a mother and her baby attempt to outrun the man-eating beasts but are cornered at a raging waterfall. With no other option available, the mother jumps, securely cradling her baby. She is mortally injured in the fall but survives long enough to deposit her newborn on the riverbank. The little boy is discovered by a woolly mammoth named Manfred, a sloth named Sid, and a saber-toothed tiger named Diego. These three unlikely companions unite on a common mission to return the baby to his father.

As the trio treks through a mountainous terrain of ice and snow while carrying the baby, at one point the mammoth, sloth, and tiger realize they're on an erupting volcano. The heat of the lava melts the glacier bridges atop the ice fields, separating Diego from the others. Isolated on a quickly melting island of ice, Diego jumps to reach the others, but he falls short. Dangling from the edge of the ice field, his grip falters, and he falls. Manfred, unwilling to let Diego perish, leaps into a chasm after him and tosses the tiger upwards to safety. Diego, realizing the danger involved in the rescue, is moved by Manfred's compassion, courage, and sacrifice.

"Why did you do that?" he asks. "You could have died trying to save me."

Humbly, the mammoth responds, "That's what you do when you're part of a herd. You look after each other."

Amazed at the convergence of circumstances that has brought these three together, Sid muses aloud. "I don't know about you guys, but we are one strange herd."

Elapsed time: Measured from the beginning of the opening credit, this scene begins at 00:53:29 and lasts about two minutes.

Content: Rated PG

Citation: *Ice Age* (20th Century Fox, 2002), written by Peter Ackerman, directed by Chris Wedge

submitted by Greg Asimakoupoulos, Naperville, Illinois

15. CIRCUMSTANCES AND FAITH

Pearl Harbor

Topic: *President Says Impossible Mission Can Be Done*

Texts: *Genesis 18:14; Matthew 17:20; Matthew 19:26; Mark 10:27; Mark 11:20–24; Luke 1:37; 2 Corinthians 5:7; Ephesians 3:20*

Keywords: *Belief; Circumstances and Faith; Confidence; Courage; Disabilities; Faith; Hardship; Hope; Leadership; Miracles; Overcoming; Prayer; Trials; Trust; Vision; Weakness*

Pearl Harbor, a movie that blends history and fiction, is about the Japanese attack on Hawaii's Pearl Harbor on December 7, 1941. Following the attack on Pearl Harbor, President Roosevelt (played by Jon Voight), seated in his wheelchair, gathers his Cabinet in the War Room of the White House. He is desperate for answers on how the United States can strike back. He speaks to the gathered advisers: "We're on the ropes, gentlemen. That's why we have to strike back now. I'm talking about hitting the heart of Japan the way they have hit us."

The head of the Army counters his chief executive. "Mr. President, Pearl Harbor caught us unawares. We didn't face the facts. This isn't a time for ignoring them again. The Army Air Corps has long-range bombers but no place to launch them. Midway is too far, and Russia won't allow us to launch a raid from there."

The president asks the head of the Navy for his opinion. The admiral is cautious, and again the president is disappointed. Frustrated that his key advisers are unwilling to take risks, President Roosevelt looks over their faces and then says: "Gentlemen, most of you did not know me when I had the use of my legs. I was young and proud and arrogant. Now I wonder every hour of my life why God put me in this chair. But when I see defeat in the eyes of my countrymen—in your eyes right now—I start to think that maybe he brought me down for times like these when we all need to be reminded who we are, that we will not give up or give in."

A decorated general speaks up. "Mr. President, with all due respect, what you're asking can't be done."

Roosevelt stares back in defiance and without saying a word struggles to pull himself with his braced legs out of his wheelchair. He pushes aside the aide who attempts to help him. At last, exhausted, he stands.

He looks at his advisers and declares, "Do not tell me it can't be done!"

Elapsed time: This scene begins at 02:10:45 and ends at 02:12:15.

Content: Rated PG-13 for battle scenes, images of the wounded, sensuality, and some language

Citation: *Pearl Harbor* (Touchstone Pictures, 2001), written by Randall Wallace, directed by Michael Bay

submitted by Greg Asimakoupoulos, Naperville, Illinois

16. COMPASSION

Out of Africa

Topic: *Seeking Welfare of the Powerless*

Texts: *Psalm 106:23; Ezekiel 22:30; John 10:15–18; Philippians 2:7–8; Hebrews 12:2*

Keywords: *Christlikeness; Compassion; Human Help; Humility; Intercession; Justice; Leadership; Love; Mercy; Perseverance; Persistence; Possessions; Support*

Out of Africa is based on the true story of Karen Blixen-Finecke (played by Meryl Streep), a wealthy Danish woman who leaves her country to buy and run a large coffee plantation in Kenya, a British colony, during the early twentieth century.

One evening she awakes to find her farm ablaze. Machines to process the coffee beans and sacks of coffee are on fire. The baroness and several dozen native workers stare helplessly. Without insurance, the baroness has no way of rebuilding her industry and must leave the country. Before she goes, however, she is determined to find land for the natives who once worked for her.

Shortly before she must return, the baroness attends a party for the new governor of Kenya (played by Leslie Phillips). While there, the governor takes her hand and says, "Baroness, I'm sorry to know that Kenya will be losing you."

"You have heard of my trouble then," the baroness replies.

"Yes. I regret it," he confesses.

"And do you know of my problem now?" she inquires.

The aide attempts to interrupt her, but the governor says, "This land you want from us—"

"Will you help me, Sir Joseph?" she implores.

Governor Joseph hedges, insisting, "That's quite difficult."

Suddenly the baroness gets down on both knees, while the political entourage protests. "Get up, Baroness. Please," the governor orders as guests begin to stare.

The baroness continues to implore him, saying, "Kenya is a hard country for women. So there is a chivalry here, of a sort. You are a powerful man, and I have no one else to turn to. You mustn't be embarrassed. I've lost everything. It costs me very little to beg you. This land was theirs, you see. We took it. And now they've nowhere else to go."

"I'll look into it. We'll do the best we can," he says and puts out his hand.

She takes his hand and asks, "May I have your word, sir?"

The governor hesitates. His wife stands up and says, "You have mine." The two women shake hands, and she is escorted from the room.

Elapsed time: Measured from the beginning of the opening credit, this scene begins at 02:11:35 and ends at 02:16:30.

Content: Rated PG

Citation: *Out of Africa* (Universal Pictures, 1985), written by Isak Dinesen and Kurt Luedtke (based on *Out of Africa* and other writings by Isak Dinesen [pen name for Karen Blixen-Finecke]), directed by Sydney Pollack

submitted by Jerry De Luca,
Montreal West, Quebec, Canada

17. COMPASSION

Walking Across Egypt

Topic: *Widow Helps Delinquent Teen*

Texts: *Matthew 25:34–40; Hebrews 13:2; James 1:27; James 2:5–8*

Keywords: *Compassion; Golden Rule; Good Deeds; Love for Christ; Mercy; Ministry; Perseverance; Persistence; Quitting; Scripture; Teenagers; Youth*

Walking Across Egypt is about a widow, Mattie Rigsby (played by Ellen Burstyn), who, moved by her pastor's message to care for "the least of these," reaches out to a sixteen-year-old boy, Wesley Benfield (played by Jonathan Taylor Thomas), whose parents abandoned him as a baby and who is serving time in a correctional center for stealing a car.

After Mattie visits Wesley at the correctional center on a couple of occasions, he breaks out and goes to her house. Thinking he is on leave, she allows him to stay with her for a short period. Ultimately, he is apprehended and returned to the center. Mattie's compassion grows for the orphan, though Mattie's adult children, Robert and Elaine, are disgruntled with her involvement with Wesley. They adamantly try to dissuade Mattie from caring for him.

Elaine argues, "He's an escaped convict. You could be charged with aiding and abetting a criminal."

Mattie snaps back, "He's not a criminal, Elaine."

Robert disagrees. "He's a thief, Mama. He's a juvenile delinquent."

Mattie says, "Robert, nobody ever loved him."

Robert replies, "If they did, he probably stole their car."

When Mattie begins to say, "The Bible says—," Elaine interjects, "We know what the Bible says. The Bible is full of wonderful stories, Mama. It is a monument to humanity, but that's all it is—it's just a storybook."

"The good Lord says we must help the least of these thy brethren," Mattie declares. "That boy is one of the least of these."

"I'll say!" Robert growls.

"You have already done plenty for him. You have done more than most would. Doesn't the Bible say when to stop?" Elaine asks.

Mattie makes an emphatic reply: "No!"

Elapsed time: Measured from the beginning of the opening credit, this scene begins at 01:33:52 and ends at 01:34:50.

Content: Rated PG-13 for violence and language

Citation: *Walking Across Egypt* (Mitchum Entertainment, 1999), written by Paul Tamasy (based on the novel by Clyde Edgerton), directed by Arthur Allan Seidelman

submitted by Van Morris, Mount Washington, Kentucky

18. COMPROMISE

Nuremberg

Topic: *Compromising Morality for the Job*

Texts: *Proverbs 1:10–18; Daniel 4:27; Matthew 25:41–45; Luke 12:4–5; Romans 9:1–5; James 4:8*

Keywords: *Career; Character; Compromise; Explanations for Evil; Integrity; Israel and Jewish Religion; Money; Morality; Self-Justification; Work*

Nuremberg, a made-for-television miniseries based on the book *Nuremberg: Infamy on Trial* by Joseph Persico, is about a series of trials held in Nuremberg, Germany, in 1945–46, in which former Nazi leaders were tried as war criminals by the International Military Tribunal.

In this scene, Nazi defendant Hans Frank (played by Frank Moore) is attempting to explain his actions to Army psychologist Gustav Gilbert (played by Matt Craven).

Frank explains, "I turned my diaries over to the Americans voluntarily. You see, they prove that I tried to resign as governor-general of Poland. I did not approve of the persecution of the Jews. Anyone reading my diaries, they will know what was in my heart. They will understand that such things I wrote about Jews, the orders I signed, they were not sincere."

"I believe you, Frank," says Gilbert, "and yet, you did do those things. How do you explain it? I don't mean legally; I'm not a lawyer or a judge. I mean how do you explain it to yourself?"

"I don't know," replies Frank. "It's as though I am two people: the Hans Frank you see here, and Hans Frank the Nazi leader. I wonder how the other Frank could do such things. This Frank looks at that Frank and says, 'You're a terrible man.'"

"And what does that Frank say back?" asks Gilbert.

Frank, appearing to plead for understanding, replies, "He says, 'I just wanted to keep my job.'"

Elapsed time: Measured from the Warner Brothers logo, this scene begins at 00:51:50 and ends at 00:53:32.

Content: Not rated. It does contain some profanity and graphic scenes from actual concentration camps.

Citation: *Nuremberg* (Cypress Films, 2000), written by David W. Rintels (based on the book by Joseph E. Persico), directed by Yves Simoneau

submitted by Van Morris, Mount Washington, Kentucky

19. CONFESSION

A Christmas Story

Topic: *Avoiding Confession*

Texts: *Psalm 32:5; Psalm 38:18; Hosea 5:15; Hebrews 9:27; Hebrews 10:22; James 5:16; 1 John 1:8–10*

Keywords: *Confession; Guilt; Judgment; Remorse; Restoration; Shame; Sin*

In *A Christmas Story*, several children gather at a school playground on a snowy day. One child tells a story about a kid who got his tongue stuck to the flagpole, adding that the fire department had to come to the scene. On a triple dog dare, one of the children, Flick (played by Scott Schwartz), agrees to put his tongue on the flagpole—and it actually sticks. Flick screams, "Stuck! Stuck! Stuck!" All the children abandon Flick, retreating into the warm classroom.

As class is about to begin, the teacher realizes Flick is missing. She inquires as to his whereabouts, but no one confesses. Finally one girl points out the window. The teacher recoils in horror as she sees Flick's tongue frozen to the pole. Eventually firemen and police extricate Flick from his predicament.

Flick somberly walks into the room with a bandaged tongue, and the teacher addresses the class with a shaming tone: "Now, I know that some of you put Flick up to this, but he has refused to say who. But those who did it know their blame, and I'm sure that the guilt you feel is far worse than any punishment you might receive. Now don't you feel terrible? Don't you feel remorse for what you've done? That's all I'm going to say about poor Flick."

Still, no one confesses. Everyone sits silently, but we hear Ralphie (the main character, played by Peter Billingsley) as he silently muses: *Adults loved to say stuff like that, but kids knew better. Kids knew darn well it was always better not to get caught.*

Elapsed time: Measured from the beginning of the opening credit, this scene begins at 00:18:01 and ends at 00:21:00.

Content: Rated PG for profanity

Citation: *A Christmas Story* (MGM, 1983), written by Leigh Brown, Bob Clark, and Jean Shepherd (based on Shepherd's *In God We Trust, All Others Pay Cash*), directed by Bob Clark

submitted by David Slagle, Wilmore, Kentucky

20. CONFLICT

The Sum of All Fears

Topic: *Resolving Conflict*

Texts: *Romans 12:16–19; 1 Corinthians 14:33; 1 Peter 3:8–14*

Keywords: *Conflict; Divisions; Leadership; Marriage; Peace; Peacemakers; Pride; Relationships; Strife*

Set in the Cold War era, *The Sum of All Fears* captures how a neo-Nazi group stages a nuclear attack in Baltimore as a way to get the Soviet Union and United States to destroy each other. Guided by misinformation and distrust, the U.S. and Russia are proud and boast their supremacy with aggressive responses until finally they are at the brink of total nuclear war.

Even though disaster is minutes away, the U.S. and Russian presidents refuse to communicate on the hot line that was designed for such situations. Jack Ryan (played by Ben Affleck), a CIA analyst, discovers crucial information about the attack and manages to access the hot line.

Since the U.S. president (played by James Cromwell) won't pull back his orders to strike, Ryan tries to convince the Russian president (played by Ciarán Hinds) to avert World War III. He informs him of the facts, emphasizing that there is another enemy, and it's the neo-Nazis trying to pit the Russians against the Americans. Ultimately, the Russian president knows he must make a crucial decision. Across the hot line screen flashes the dramatic end to the conversation:

"What are you asking of me?" the Russian president asks.

"Back down," Ryan writes.

"What guarantee do I have that President Fowler will follow suit?"

"None," Ryan responds.

Russian generals hiss at the president to launch the nuclear devices immediately. They're convinced Ryan is a quack. But Ryan finishes his dramatic monologue: "It no longer has anything to do with Baltimore. It has to do with fear. Our fear of your missiles and your fear of our subs."

Finally, after a tense pause, the Russian president states, "On my order, all Russian strategic forces are standing down. We will maintain a defensive alert for the moment, but our offensive forces are withdrawn. If you match our move, I propose a phased mutual stand-down."

With great relief, the U.S. president immediately follows suit.

This scene captures crucial biblical teaching about conflict. First, there is often a third party involved—Satan, the true enemy—who is seeking our mutual destruction. Second, conflicts soon become less about the original events and more about fear and distrust. Third, the courage to cease aggression without promises is the path to peace.

Elapsed time: Measured from the beginning of the opening credit, this scene begins at 01:48:00 and ends at about 01:49:00. Caution: Soon after this scene, Jack Ryan uses profanity.

Content: Rated PG-13 for profanity, violence, and sexual content

Citation: *The Sum of All Fears* (Paramount Pictures, 2002), written by Paul Attanasio and Daniel Pyne (based on the novel by Tom Clancy), directed by Phil Alden Robinson

submitted by Bill White, Paramount, California

21. CONVERSION

A Walk to Remember

Topic: *Miracle of Conversion*

Texts: *Mark 5:15; John 3:5–8; John 9:25; Romans 12:1–8; Ephesians 2:4–10*

Keywords: *Change; Conversion; Influence; Inspiration of Persons; Love; Miracles; Salvation*

Based on the novel by Nicholas Sparks, *A Walk to Remember* illustrates how one person's life and death can have a positive impact on an entire community. Jamie Sullivan (played by Mandy Moore) is the high school daughter of a widowed minister in the small town of Beaufort, North Carolina. Though she is ridiculed by the "in crowd" for her conservative appearance and values, Jamie resolves to be her own person. The high school yearbook calls attention to her primary ambition in life: "To witness a miracle."

Jamie is dying of leukemia. When Jamie befriends Landon Carter (played by Shane West), one of those who's been mocking her, her father and Landon's friends are concerned. But Jamie pours her life into Landon, helping him study, rallying him to memorize his lines for a school play, and introducing him to the wonder of astronomy. During this time frame, Landon falls in love with Jamie.

Eventually they marry. After a mere three months, Jamie dies. In honor of Jamie, Landon decides to attend college, where he distinguishes himself as a capable student. After graduation, he returns home to Beaufort. The first person he wants to see is Jamie's father (played by Peter Coyote).

As the two sit down, Landon announces he's been accepted into medical school.

Landon reaches into his backpack and pulls out a book of poetry and quotes that had originally belonged to Jamie's mom, but which Jamie had given to Landon when she had been sick.

"I want you to have it," Landon says to Reverend Sullivan, handing him the dog-eared volume.

Landon says, "I'm sorry she never got her miracle."

The minister looks straight at Landon. "She did. It was you."

Elapsed time: Measured from the beginning of the opening credit, this scene begins at 01:34:35 and lasts approximately three minutes.

Content: Rated PG for mild profanity and some sensual elements

Citation: *A Walk to Remember* (Warner Brothers, 2002), written by Karen Janszen (based on the novel by Nicholas Sparks), directed by Adam Shankman

submitted by Greg Asimakoupoulos, Naperville, Illinois

22. COVETING

King George and the Ducky

Topic: *Never Content*

Texts: *Exodus 20:17; 2 Samuel 11:1–5; Ecclesiastes 5:10; Luke 12:13–34; Ephesians 5:3; 1 Timothy 6:6; Hebrews 13:5–6; James 4:1–4*

Keywords: *Contentment; Coveting; Covetousness; Desire; Discontent; Greed; Materialism; Satisfaction; Self-Centeredness; Selfishness*

In VeggieTales' *King George and the Ducky,* an adaptation of the story of David and Bathsheba, Larry the Cucumber stars as King George, and Bob the Tomato is his faithful servant Lewis. The privileges of royalty—kingdom expansion, castles, power, and treasures—do not appeal to King George. But King George loves to bathe with his rubber duck. Splishing and splashing, he sings an ode to his rubber duck called—what else?—"I Love My Duck."

One day while standing on the royal balcony in his purple robe and golden crown, King George peers through binoculars, and his eyes grow wide with desire. He spies something wonderful—a rubber duck. But it belongs to Billy, who happens to be bathing with his rubber duck on his own balcony. Billy's rubber duck looks exactly like King George's rubber duck. Nonetheless, the king covets it, exclaiming, "I want it."

Lewis reminds him that he already has a duck and that the other duck belongs to someone else.

"Are you saying I shouldn't have whatever I want?" asks the king.

Lewis opens a large wardrobe overflowing with hundreds of identical rubber ducks and says, "If I could just jog your memory, you already have quite a few ducks."

King George's rationale is simple. He shoots a condescending look at his unlearned servant and replies, "Those are *yesterday's* ducks."

Elapsed time: Measured from the beginning of the opening credit, this scene starts at 00:13:29 and ends at 00:16:04.

Content: Not rated

Citation: *King George and the Ducky* (Big Idea Productions, 2000), written by Phil Vischer, directed by Mike Nawrocki

submitted by David Slagle, Wilmore, Kentucky

23. DEVOTION

The Color Purple

Topic: *Family Devotion*

Texts: *Romans 8:35–39; Romans 12:10;
1 Corinthians 13:4–8*

Keywords: *Commitment; Communication;
Determination; Devotion; Family; Love; Loyalty;
Promises; Relationships*

The Color Purple, based on Alice Walker's Pulitzer Prize-winning novel, tells the story of a girl named Celie (played by Whoopi Goldberg), who grows up in the rural South.

Fourteen-year-old Celie is forced to marry Albert Johnson (played by Danny Glover), a widower farmer who treats his teenage bride more like a slave than a wife. When Celie's sister, Nettie (played by Akosua Busia), comes for a visit, they share hours of laughter and companionship. Celie is delighted when Albert agrees to let Nettie move in as part of the family.

As Nettie is walking to school, however, Albert stalks her through the trees with wrong intentions. When he attacks her, Nettie fights him off, kicking him in the groin. While he writhes in pain, she runs back to the house to tell Celie what happened.

When Albert returns, Celie shields Nettie from her incensed husband. Through a veil of tears and screams, she pleads with Albert to let her sister stay. Albert's children cease their play near the barn and look on in horror.

Albert pushes Celie off and begins to chase Nettie off the land. Celie grabs her husband's legs to try and stop him. Dragging Celie behind him, he reaches the end of the property line and throws stones at Nettie, who is weeping as she stumbles down the road.

Celie calls out, "Write me, Nettie! Write!"

Nettie stops in her tracks and turns around. After looking defiantly at Albert, she shifts her glance toward her sister and shouts, "Nothing but death will keep me from it."

Elapsed time: This scene begins at 00:25:25 and lasts about three minutes.

Content: Rated PG-13 for violence and adult situations

Citation: *The Color Purple* (Warner Brothers, 1985), written by Menno Meyjes (based on the novel by Alice Walker), directed by Steven Spielberg

submitted by Greg Asimakoupoulos, Naperville, Illinois

24. DISCONTENT

The Big Chill

Topic: *Disillusionment with Life's Dreams*

Texts: *Psalm 127:1–2; Jeremiah 2:5;
Jeremiah 51:58; Romans 1:21;
1 Corinthians 3:19–20; Ephesians
4:17–18; 1 Timothy 6:6–8*

Keywords: *Boredom; Confusion; Decisions; Disappoint-
ments; Discontent; Dreams; Emptiness; Expectations;
Family; Frustration; Goals; Insecurity; Marriage;
Motherhood; Priorities; Purpose; Reflection; Regret;
Self-Examination; Uncertainties*

The Big Chill is about eight college friends who reunite years later for the funeral of one of their buddies. They reflect on their current lives and how their 1960s ideas and hopes compare with the realities of their 1980s lives.

Sam (played by Tom Berenger), a successful actor, and Karen (played by JoBeth Williams), a housewife and mother, are on a pier overlooking a watery marsh. Sam says to Karen that she and her husband have "really built something for yourselves, I'll bet." Karen explains that Richard is the kind of stable husband and father her own father wasn't as she was growing up. "It's just that now—well—you know . . ." She sighs and sits down. Sam urges her to share her feelings and sits next to her.

Karen explains, "All my life, deep inside, I've felt that there was something that I really wanted to express, but I've always felt, I don't know, stymied. But I'm proud of what I did. I'm doing a good job of raising my sons. And if it meant that I had to give up my writing, well, that's the way it goes. But what's the use of talking about it? I've made my decision. My children come first. It's just that now, it leaves kind of a—a space. And all of Richard's country clubs and home improvements and business . . . (sighs) Pretty superficial stuff. I'm not complaining. Well, maybe I am."

Elapsed time: This scene begins at 01:07:25 and ends at 01:09:17.

Content: Rated R for language and themes

Citation: *The Big Chill* (Columbia Pictures, 1983), written by Barbara Benedek and Lawrence Kasdan, directed by Lawrence Kasdan

submitted by Jerry De Luca,
Montreal West, Quebec, Canada

Stepmom

Topic: *Putting Feelings before Commitment*

Texts: *Matthew 19:4–6; Mark 10:2–12*

Keywords: *Attitudes and Emotions; Children; Commitment; Conflict; Divorce; Emotions; Faithfulness; Family; Marriage; Promises; Relationships*

Stepmom, starring Julia Roberts and Susan Sarandon, is about the strained relationship between a new stepmother and her husband's ex-wife. Both must learn to accept one another in their new roles, especially as they both attempt to raise the ex-wife's two young children.

At the start of this scene, Luke (played by Ed Harris) brings his two children, Anna (played by Jena Malone), age twelve, and Benjamin (played by Liam Aiken), age eight, to a park where remote-controlled sailboats are being sailed. As Luke and Benjamin launch their sailboat, Anna, looking sad, asks why Luke's new wife, Isabel (played by Julia Roberts), has moved in with them. Momentarily surprised at the question, Luke answers, "Because we love each other. And we want to share our lives together."

"We already had a life together with Mommy," Anna replies.

"But Mommy and I weren't getting along very well. And it wasn't fair to you guys, fighting all the time."

Benjamin interjects, "I fight with Anna all the time. Can I move out?"

Luke smiles and says, "No, but you guys are brother and sister."

"You were husband and wife," says Anna. "Doesn't that mean something?"

Luke, caught off guard, slowly says, "Yes. It does. But, well, when you get older, your relationships get a lot more complicated. And there's all kinds of feelings flying around. And sometimes some of those feelings change."

Anna then asks, "But did you fall out of love with Mommy?"

"Well, yeah, I guess I did. I still love your mom. But it just became a different kind of love, that's all. We're still really good friends, and we always will be."

Benjamin asks with a serious look, "Can you ever fall out of love with your kids?"

Elapsed time: This scene begins at 00:15:35 and ends at 00:17:39.

Content: Rated PG-13 for language and thematic elements

Citation: *Stepmom* (Columbia TriStar, 1998), written by Gigi Levangie, directed by Chris Columbus

submitted by Jerry De Luca,
Montreal West, Quebec, Canada

26. ENDURANCE

Band of Brothers
Episode 6: Bastogne

Topic: *Staying on the Front Line*

Texts: *2 Corinthians 1:8–10; 2 Corinthians 11:16–33; Ephesians 6:10–13; 2 Timothy 2:3; 2 Timothy 4:6–8*

Keywords: *Courage; Determination; Endurance; Hardship; Long-Suffering; Ministry; Perseverance; Persistence; Servanthood; Spiritual Warfare; Unselfishness*

The miniseries *Band of Brothers* is the story of Easy Company, a United States Army Airborne paratrooper division, and their World War II operations in Europe. The miniseries was based on historian Stephen Ambrose's nonfiction book *Band of Brothers*.

In episode 6, Easy Company finds itself surrounded, cold, and short on ammunition and winter gear near the Belgian town of Bastogne, a crucial position in the Allied defensive line during the Battle of the Bulge (December 1944 to January 1945).

Eugene Roe, one of three company medics, is scampering around to save lives—scrounging for morphine, scissors, and bandages. While Easy Company is dug in and holding the front line, Roe (played by Shane Taylor) discovers Joe Toye (played by Kirk Acevedo) sitting in his foxhole with his boots off in the dead of winter. Roe looks at Joe's limp, discolored, and frostbitten feet and tells Joe that he could get gangrene and lose them.

In this condition, Joe could have been taken off the front line to a warm bed, but instead he looks cold-eyed at Roe and says, "I ain't coming off the line, Doc."

(Toye later lost his right leg when he was hit by a barrage of enemy fire while shouting for the men in his company to take cover in their foxholes. Toye was awarded the Silver Star for his service. Easy Company went on to make it all the way to Adolf Hitler's mountain-top retreat, Eagle's Nest.)

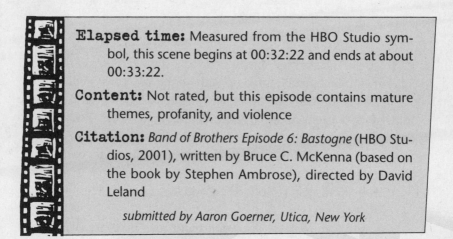

Elapsed time: Measured from the HBO Studio symbol, this scene begins at 00:32:22 and ends at about 00:33:22.

Content: Not rated, but this episode contains mature themes, profanity, and violence

Citation: *Band of Brothers Episode 6: Bastogne* (HBO Studios, 2001), written by Bruce C. McKenna (based on the book by Stephen Ambrose), directed by David Leland

submitted by Aaron Goerner, Utica, New York

27. EVANGELISM

The Good Girl

Topic: *How Not to Evangelize*

Texts: *Matthew 28:18–20; John 20:21–23; Acts 1:8*

Keywords: *Evangelism; Witness; Witnessing*

The Good Girl stars Jennifer Aniston as Justine Last, a thirty-year-old small-town girl who is fed up with her boring job at Retail Rodeo.

In one scene early in the movie, Justine is approached by Corny (played by Mike White), a security guard at Retail Rodeo, who demonstrates perhaps the best way not to evangelize.

Corny: "Hey Justine, can I talk with you for just a second?"

Justine: "Yeah."

Corny: "I was just curious. Have you ever been to a Bible study?"

Justine: "Yeah."

Corny: "Yeah, well we got a good one goin' on every Wednesday at the First Church of the Nazarene. Rodney comes. Benita comes. You got any interest in readin' the Bible?"

Justine: "I have—I have my own, you know, beliefs."

Corny: "Well, we don't preach fire and brimstone. Ten Commandments, gotta live by those. Other than the usual ways we're not interested in scaring people. We're about lovin' Jesus."

Justine: "Uh huh. Yeah, I kinda like my nights to myself."

Corny: "Well, maybe you'll have night after night of eternal hell-fire all to yourself. Just kidding ya. Drive safe."

Justine: (stunned) "Bye-bye."

Elapsed time: Measured from the Fox Searchlight Pictures logo, this scene begins at 00:02:50 and ends at 00:03:35.

Content: Rated R for sexuality, language, and drug content

Citation: *The Good Girl* (Fox Searchlight Pictures, 2002), written by Mike White, directed by Miguel Arteta

submitted by Van Morris, Mount Washington, Kentucky

28. EXPECTATIONS

Singles

Topic: *Lowering Standards for a Mate*

Texts: *Romans 5:5; 1 Corinthians 7:32–35; Ephesians 3:14–21*

Keywords: *Companionship; Dating; Disappointments; Expectations; Marriage; Relationships; Romance; Romantic Love*

Singles portrays a group of twenty-somethings looking for love. Theirs is an unending search for a true companion, which seems forever out of reach.

At one point, Janet (played by Bridget Fonda) considers plastic surgery to make herself more attractive. Her friend Steve (played by Campbell Scott) accompanies her to the doctor's office.

As they sit in the waiting room, Steve asks, "Tell me, from a girl's point of view, what do you really want from a guy?"

Janet says, "Well, when I first moved out here from Arizona, I wanted a guy with looks, security, who's caring, someone with their own place, someone who said bless you or gesundheit when I sneezed, you know, and someone who liked the same things as me but not exactly. Someone who loves me."

"That's a tall order."

"Yeah, I scaled it down a little."

"Well, what is it now?" Steve asks.

"Someone who says gesundheit when I sneeze, although I prefer bless you. It's nicer."

Elapsed time: This scene begins at 00:51:00 and ends at 00:52:00.

Content: Rated PG-13 for adult situations and profanity

Citation: *Singles* (Warner Brothers, 1992) written and directed by Cameron Crowe

submitted by Bill White, Paramount, California

29. FAILURE

My Dog Skip

Topic: *Overcoming Failure*

Texts: *Proverbs 17:17; Matthew 26:31–35; John 8:2–11; Galatians 6:1; James 5:19–20*

Keywords: *Cowardice; Failure; Friendship; Heroes; Human Faithfulness; Judging Others; Judgment; Restoration; Shame*

My Dog Skip is based on the childhood of American writer Willie Morris. It chronicles life-lessons learned from a beloved terrier and a next-door neighbor, as well as from the disappointments that flow out of a world at war.

Small for his age and bullied by other kids, Willie (played by Frankie Muniz) enjoys a special relationship with eighteen-year-old Dink Jenkins (played by Luke Wilson), who lives next door. But when Dink is drafted to fight the Nazis in Europe, Willie feels as though he's lost his only friend in the world. His parents buy him a terrier puppy (named Skip) to compensate for his loss, and the dog becomes his constant companion.

Still, when Willie hears that Dink has returned from the war, he can't wait to spend time with his hero. When he discovers that Dink disgraced himself as a deserter and has resorted to alcohol as a means of drowning his shame, Willie is devastated. He can't understand why Dink doesn't want to spend time with him anymore.

When Skip gets lost, Dink tries to comfort Willie and helps him think of one place he hasn't looked yet. As the boy races off to look,

Willie's dad (played by Kevin Bacon), who lost his leg in the Battle of the Bulge, awkwardly limps down the front steps and engages his shunned neighbor in conversation. Aware of how Dink is shamed by his failure, Mr. Morris tries to convince him that people's opinions will fade in time.

Dink eyes him and says, "You got a purple heart. I've got a yellow stripe. You can trust me, they don't forget about cowards."

With empathy, Mr. Morris says, "Well, folks like to keep things small, Dink. Fit you into one pocket or the other. Give a man a label, and you never really need to get to know him. My son looks up to you, Dink. Not because you can run or throw a ball. You're his hero because you're his friend. That's what he needs. A friend."

There is an awkward silence. Dink looks down at the ground, ashamed of how he has failed his friend but challenged by Mr. Morris's words, knowing it's not too late to begin anew.

Elapsed time: This scene begins at 01:16:16 and ends at about 01:17:46.

Content: Rated PG for some violence and language

Citation: *My Dog Skip* (Warner Brothers, 1999), written by Gail Gilchriest (based on the book by Willie Morris), directed by Jay Russell

submitted by Greg Asimakoupoulos, Naperville, Illinois

The Lord of the Rings: The Fellowship of the Ring

Topic: *A Faithful Friend*

Texts: *Deuteronomy 31:6; Ruth 1:16–18; 1 Samuel 18:1–4; Proverbs 18:24; Matthew 14:25–33; Matthew 26:31–35; Romans 12:10; Galatians 5:22; 2 Timothy 1:16–18*

Keywords: *Devotion; Faithfulness; Friendship; Loyalty; Promises; Relationships*

In *The Lord of the Rings: The Fellowship of the Ring*, Frodo Baggins (played by Elijah Wood), a hobbit, is given the unenviable task of destroying a ring in The Cracks of Doom in a dark and evil land called Mordor. His task is fraught with mortal danger.

Gandalf the wizard (played by Ian McKellen) understands such a perilous journey could cause anyone to become discouraged. Gandalf encourages Frodo's best friend, Samwise Gamgee (played by Sean Astin), to accompany Frodo on the trip. In fact, Gandalf makes Samwise promise he will never leave Frodo. Several other brave individuals accompany Frodo as well. These nine travelers become the "Fellowship of the Ring."

Well into the journey, the lives of those in the Fellowship have been endangered on multiple occasions. Concerned for the safety of his friends, Frodo makes a private and noble decision to slip away from his friends and make the remainder of the journey on his own. Frodo steps into a boat and quietly pushes away from the shore.

Suddenly the branches on the sloping hill above the shore begin to snap and give way to a tiny hobbit warrior. Samwise Gamgee crashes through the branches and onto the shore, shouting, "Frodo! Mr. Frodo!"

Frodo yells back, "Go back, Sam! I'm going to Mordor alone!"

Sam is not deterred. He continues toward Frodo, splashing into the river up to his waist. "Of course you are, and I'm coming with you!"

"You can't swim!" Frodo shouts. "Sam! Sam!"

Sam tries desperately to swim out to the boat. Frodo watches as Sam begins to sink beneath the murky surface of the river.

Frodo reaches down and grabs Sam's wrist, pulling him up and into the boat. Frodo looks at Sam as if to say, *Why? Why would you risk your life attempting to swim out to me?*

A soaking-wet Sam sees the question in Frodo's eyes and says, "I made a promise, Mr. Frodo. A promise. 'Don't you leave him, Samwise Gamgee.' And I don't mean to. I don't mean to."

Frodo embraces Sam. "Come on," he smiles.

Elapsed time: This scene begins at 02:45:25 and ends at 02:47:37.

Content: Rated PG-13 for epic battle sequences and scary images

Citation: *The Lord of the Rings: The Fellowship of the Ring* (New Line Cinema, 2001), written by Philippa Boyens, Peter Jackson, and Fran Walsh (based on the novel by J. R .R. Tolkien), directed by Peter Jackson

submitted by David Slagle, Wilmore, Kentucky

31. FAMILY

Antwone Fisher

Topic: *Finding a Welcome in God's Family*

Texts: *Isaiah 25:6; Isaiah 61:1–3; Revelation 19:7–9*

Keywords: *Acceptance; Belonging; Church; Community; Family; Feasts; Fellowship; God's Kingdom; Grace; Heaven; Hope*

Antwone Fisher is the true story of a young man abandoned at birth by an incarcerated woman and raised in abusive orphanages, foster homes, and reform schools. After his eighteenth birthday, he joins the United States Navy, where his anger toward life brims to the surface. After several fights, he is ordered to undergo counseling. Psychologist Jerome Davenport (played by Denzel Washington) encourages Antwone (played by Derek Luke) to find his roots to begin healing.

After several phone calls, he reaches an aunt and uncle in Cleveland, who escort him to a dilapidated apartment complex where his estranged mother lives. A suspicious and aloof woman answers the door. Upon realizing that Antwone is the child she gave up at birth, she retreats to another room and sits down on a soiled, worn couch and cries silently.

Antwone asks for some explanation as to why she never came to rescue him or why she never sought him out. She cannot answer. She simply stares ahead, not daring to look at him, tears rolling down her expressionless face.

He gently kisses her on the cheek as if to say, "I forgive you," and walks away. His mother remains on the couch and stares at nothing, making no effort to respond. A despondent Fisher leaves the apartment with his questions unanswered and rides back to his aunt's house with his uncle.

As he exits the car, his slow gait betrays the loneliness of a man with no hope of a meaningful connection to anyone. As Antwone enters the front door, however, his world changes. He is met with a chorus of cheers from more than fifty relatives, all waiting to meet Antwone for the first time.

There are children, couples, cousins, uncles, aunts, and family friends, all smothering him with hugs, slaps on the back, and beaming smiles. One cousin gives his name as Edward and says, "I'm named after your dad," and an older aunt squeezes his cheeks. Antwone takes it all in, overwhelmed.

The hallway stairs are filled with kids holding up signs with his name scribbled next to crayola-sketched smiley faces and rainbows. He is then led into another room, where a grand feast is spread across a long table. The table is overflowing with chicken, mashed potatoes, pancakes, fruit salad, and every other possible dish. The room is prepared for a party. For the first time in his life, Antwone is being adored. For the first time, he belongs.

As the clamor quiets, an elderly woman sitting behind the table knocks to get Antwone's attention and then waves for him to come over. With slow, deliberate moves, she raises her arms, grabbing his hands and then caressing his face. A slow tear runs down her cheek, and with a raspy voice that seemed to be mustering all the strength it possessed, she whispered the redemptive invitation: "Welcome."

In much the same way, we are welcome in the family of God.

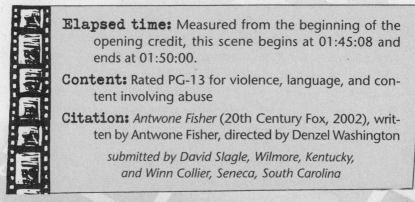

Elapsed time: Measured from the beginning of the opening credit, this scene begins at 01:45:08 and ends at 01:50:00.

Content: Rated PG-13 for violence, language, and content involving abuse

Citation: *Antwone Fisher* (20th Century Fox, 2002), written by Antwone Fisher, directed by Denzel Washington

*submitted by David Slagle, Wilmore, Kentucky,
and Winn Collier, Seneca, South Carolina*

32. FAMILY OF GOD

Lilo & Stitch

Topic: *In Families, No One Is Forgotten*

Texts: *Romans 12:10; Romans 15:5; 1 Corinthians 13:4–8; Ephesians 4:2; Colossians 3:12–14; 1 Peter 3:8*

Keywords: *Brotherhood; Church as Family of God; Commitment; Devotion; Family; Family of God; Forgiveness; Love; Loyalty; Tolerance; Unity; Unity of the Church*

In the Disney film *Lilo & Stitch,* Stitch (voiced by Christopher Michael Sanders) is a creature from outer space. He is the result of a genetic experiment by an alien scientist. He is small, blue, and toothy. He slobbers and growls almost continually, and his genetic instinct is to destroy. Though he is no bigger than the average dog, Stitch can lift items several times his own weight, and he breaks almost everything he touches.

Stitch escapes his home planet and makes his way to earth, where he is mistaken for a dog by a young Hawaiian girl named Lilo. Lilo (voiced by Daveigh Chase) adopts Stitch from the local pound, and he becomes a member of this small, broken family.

Lilo is unlike other girls her age; she is a rough-and-tumble girl. She has been in the care of her older sister, Nani, since their parents died in a car accident. Lilo, like Stitch, doesn't fit in well. This creates a bond between the two.

Lilo and her sister soon realize they have no ordinary canine on their hands. One night at a restaurant, Stitch attempts to swallow the head of another patron. When they get home, Stitch goes into destruction mode. He blows the contents of a blender all over the kitchen and then breaks the blender. Frustrated by Stitch's behavior, Lilo's sister prepares to throw Stitch out. Stitch is saved only because of a family motto passed down from their father—the Hawaiian word *ohana*. Just as the older sister tosses Stitch out on his ear, Lilo cries, "What about *ohana*?!"

"He hasn't been here that long," says her older sister.

"I haven't either!" says Lilo. "*Ohana* means family, and in family no one gets left behind—or forgotten."

The older sister says, "I hate it when you pull *ohana* on me." Reluctantly the older sister agrees to keep Stitch.

Elapsed time: Measured from the beginning of the opening credit, this scene begins at 00:35:15 and ends at 00:36:29.

Content: Rated PG

Citation: *Lilo & Stitch* (Walt Disney Pictures, 2002), written and directed by Dean DeBlois and Chris Sanders

submitted by David Slagle, Wilmore, Kentucky

33. FEAR

Snow White and the Seven Dwarfs

Topic: *Unreasonable Fear*

Texts: *Matthew 6:25–34; Luke 12:22–26; Philippians 4:6–7*

Keywords: *Adversity; Anxiety; Fear; Peace; Problems; Trouble; Worry*

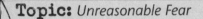

In the classic animated film *Snow White and the Seven Dwarfs,* the dwarfs return home from a hard day at the mines, their picks slung over their small shoulders. From a distance, they see that their small cabin in the woods is unexpectedly aglow, and a billow of smoke drifts from the chimney. Warily, they make their way into their cabin and discover that an intruder is asleep in their bedroom. Their imaginations run wild as they discuss what vile creature slumbers in their room.

The other dwarfs urge Dopey to go and investigate. "Don't worry. We're right behind you," they assure him. Dopey carefully cracks open the door and enters. Just then, the "thing" under the sheets stretches, and Dopey and the other dwarfs flee in unbridled terror. "What was it?" they scream. "Did you see it? Did you see it?"

Dopey nods his head vigorously.

"Was it a dragon?"

Again Dopey nods yes.

"Did it have horns?"

Using his fingers to imitate horns, Dopey nods again.

"Did it slobber?"

Dopey nods again, slobbering profusely.

The fears of the dwarfs have grown larger with each question. "What was it doing?" they ask.

Dopey closes his eyes and snores.

Doc cries, "There's a monster sleeping in our beds! Let's get him while we can."

Once again they venture up the stairs to deal with the beast in the bed. Gathering around the bed, they raise their picks to deal the fatal blow to the monster. But when the sheets are thrown back, they find a harmless guest—the young Snow White.

Elapsed time: Measured from the beginning of the opening credit, this scene begins at 00:31:22 and ends at 00:35:35.

Content: Rated G

Citation: *Snow White and the Seven Dwarfs* (Walt Disney Pictures, 1937), written by Ted Sears, Richard Creedon, Otto Englander, Dick Rickard, Earl Hurd, Merrill De Maris, Dorothy Ann Blank, and Webb Smith (based on the story by Jacob Ludwig Carl Grimm and Wilhelm Carl Grimm), directed by David Hand

submitted by David Slagle, Wilmore, Kentucky

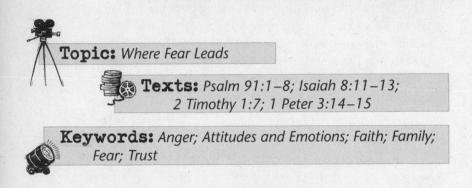

34. FEER

Star Wars Episode 1: The Phantom Menace

Topic: *Where Fear Leads*

Texts: *Psalm 91:1–8; Isaiah 8:11–13; 2 Timothy 1:7; 1 Peter 3:14–15*

Keywords: *Anger; Attitudes and Emotions; Faith; Family; Fear; Trust*

Star Wars Episode 1: The Phantom Menace begins the science-fiction epic that in later movies pits the evil Darth Vader and his imperialistic regime against all that is good in the universe. The movie centers on a young boy, Anakin Skywalker (played by Jake Lloyd), who appears to have the highly prized qualities needed to become one of the elite Jedi knights.

In this scene Anakin is being examined in front of the council of the Jedis. For him, it's the interview of a lifetime—the chance to become one of the protectors of the universe—but the interview turns out to be more revealing of his heart than he expected.

The council puts Anakin through a series of tests and then questions him about his fears. The head of the council, Yoda (voiced by Frank Oz), asks him in his strange voice, "How feel you?"

"Cold, sir," Anakin replies.

"Afraid are you?" asks Yoda.

"No, sir."

"See through you we can."

Another council member says, "Your thoughts dwell on your mother."

"I miss her," Anakin says.

"Afraid to lose her, I think," muses Yoda.

But Anakin objects, "What has that got to do with anything?"

"Everything!" Yoda suddenly insists. "Fear is the path to the Dark Side. Fear leads to anger, anger leads to hate, hate leads to suffering." Yoda pauses and sighs. "I sense much fear in you."

In later *Star Wars* movies, Anakin is afraid to let go of other things (including his mother) to pursue the calling of a Jedi. Anakin's fear of surrender leads him down that path of fear to anger to hate, until he eventually becomes *Star Wars*'s greatest villain, the evil Darth Vader.

Elapsed time: This scene begins at 01:26:00 and lasts about two minutes.

Content: Rated PG for science-fiction action and violence

Citation: *Star Wars Episode 1: The Phantom Menace* (20th Century Fox and Lucasfilm, 1999), written and directed by George Lucas

submitted by Bill White, Paramount, California

35. FEAR OF DEATH

The Royal Tenenbaums

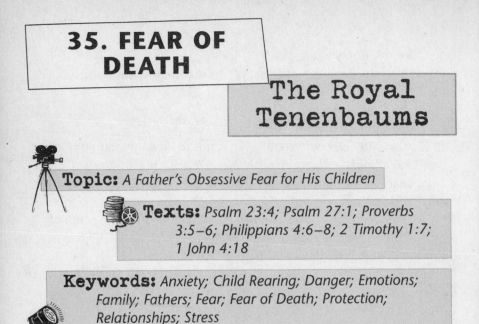

Topic: *A Father's Obsessive Fear for His Children*

Texts: *Psalm 23:4; Psalm 27:1; Proverbs 3:5–6; Philippians 4:6–8; 2 Timothy 1:7; 1 John 4:18*

Keywords: *Anxiety; Child Rearing; Danger; Emotions; Family; Fathers; Fear; Fear of Death; Protection; Relationships; Stress*

The Royal Tenenbaums is a comedic film about a dysfunctional family. Royal Tenenbaum and his wife, Etheline, have three child prodigies. One is a genius business mogul, another a Pulitzer Prize-winning playwright, and the third a championship tennis star. Because of a lack of love from their father, all three children grow up neurotic.

One of Royal's three children is Chas, the business mogul (played by Ben Stiller). Although his superintelligence has brought him economic success, he grieves inconsolably for his wife. She tragically died in a plane crash that Chas, his two sons, and the family dog survived. In light of what happened to his wife, Chas is obsessively afraid of disaster. He never lets his children out of the house for fear something will happen to them. He dresses them every day in matching red sweat suits and demands that they work out in a rooftop gym to maintain their physical readiness.

In one bizarre expression of his fear, Chas engages a fire alarm and then runs through his three-story New York town house at midnight, shouting at his boys to wake up and run out of the condo. As he races through the house like a maniac, Chas shouts, "Let's go! Go, go, go! Look alive!"

The boys, Ari and Uzi, comply. Apparently they are accustomed to these middle-of-the-night fire drills. When they emerge from their town house, Chas looks at his watch and grimly says, "Four minutes and forty-eight seconds. Not good enough. We're dead. We are all burned to a crisp."

Elapsed time: Measured from the beginning of the opening credit, this scene begins at 00:12:16 and ends at about 00:13:16.

Content: Rated R for language, sexuality/nudity, and drug use

Citation: *The Royal Tenenbaums* (Touchstone Pictures, 2001), written by Wes Anderson and Owen Wilson, directed by Wes Anderson

submitted by Greg Asimakoupoulos, Naperville, Illinois

36. FORGIVENESS

With Honors

Topic: *Father Seeks Son's Forgiveness*

Texts: *Matthew 6:12–15; Matthew 18:21–
35; Mark 11:25; Luke 6:37; Luke 11:4;
Luke 17:3–4; Colossians 3:13*

Keywords: *Anger; Apology; Bitterness; Family; Fathers;
Forgiveness; Grudges; Hardness of Heart; Hatred;
Repentance*

In *With Honors,* Joe Pesci plays the role of Simon Wilder, a homeless vagrant living in the boiler room of the Harvard University
library.

One day Simon finds the one and only copy of a senior thesis by
a Harvard student named Monty Kessler (played by Brendan Fraser).
When the panicked student discovers the whereabouts of his mis-
placed term project, he offers Simon food and shelter in exchange for
the paper. A friendship eventually emerges between this unlikely pair.

Simon explains to Monty that he has been homeless since being
fired from his job in the Baltimore shipyards. He was too sick to work.
It becomes obvious that Simon was exposed to lethal amounts of
asbestos and is terminally ill.

As he writes a draft of his own obituary, Simon confides in Monty
that he had been married at the age of twenty and had a son. He
deserted the family the year his son was born. He is ashamed, but
knowing he is near death he wants to make things right with his
grown son.

Monty and his housemates drive Simon to a farm in Maine.
Monty approaches the farmhouse and speaks to the man who

answers the door. "Mr. Wilder," Monty begins. "My name is Monty Kessler. I'm a student at Harvard. I guess it was about three months ago I met your father. He's in the van and wants to see you."

The grown son's face betrays his conflicted feelings. He responds, "I don't have a father."

Monty insists, "Please, he's very ill."

"I don't want to see him."

"But he's dying! Please just walk over for a couple minutes, say hello, and let him look at you. Then we'll go, and you'll never have to see him again."

The son reluctantly agrees. Monty escorts him to the van, where Simon has managed to sit up and has combed his hair to look as presentable as possible. The estranged father looks longingly into his son's face.

Finally the son breaks the awkward silence. "Is there something you want from me?"

"I just wanted to look at you."

"Fine. Have a look! Seen enough?"

"You look good," Simon says. "I'm your father."

With hardened hatred, the son says, "You don't look like much."

Swallowing hard, Simon manages an apology that he has mentally rehearsed for thirty years. "I was wrong. I'm sorry!"

The son interrupts him and says, "Yeah, you were wrong, and I don't care about you being sorry. And I don't care about you."

The son's preschool-age daughter approaches the van, and seeing Simon, she asks, "Daddy, who is that man?"

Still looking at his estranged father, the son says to his little girl, "He's nobody, baby. He's nobody."

Elapsed time: Measured from the beginning of the opening credit, this scene begins at 01:25:15 and lasts about four minutes.

Content: Rated PG-13 for mild profanity and sensuality

Citation: *With Honors* (Warner Brothers, 1994), written by William Mastrosimone, directed by Alek Keshishian

submitted by Greg Asimakoupoulos, Naperville, Illinois

The Lord of the Rings: The Fellowship of the Ring

Topic: *The Least Becomes Greatest*

Texts: *Psalm 110:3; Matthew 23:12; Mark 9:35; Luke 9:46–48; Luke 14:11; Luke 18:14; 1 Corinthians 1:26–31; 1 Corinthians 15:58; Philippians 2:1–10; 1 Peter 5:5–6*

Keywords: *Courage; Greatness; Humility; Leadership; Sacrifice; Servanthood; Service; Weakness*

In *The Lord of the Rings: The Fellowship of the Ring,* Christian author J. R. R. Tolkien portrays the classic conflict between good and evil, set in a mythical land called Middle Earth. After a great battle in ancient times, the Dark Lord Sauron is temporarily defeated, and his most dreaded weapon, the Ring of Power, is lost for many ages.

A character named Bilbo Baggins finds the ring and, unaware of its true identity, passes it on to his nephew Frodo as part of an inheritance. Frodo Baggins (played by Elijah Wood) plays the central role in the story—and he is an unlikely hero. Full of humility and hesitation, he embarks on an epic quest to destroy this most powerful tool of the Dark Lord.

At one point the rulers of the nations have gathered in a council to decide what to do with the ring, which sits before them on a stone pedestal. The fate of the world hangs on their decision. Under the strain of the decision and the seeming impossibility of the task, bitter infighting breaks out in the council.

"The ring was made in the fires of Mount Doom," says the head of the council. "Only there can it be unmade. It must be taken deep into Mordor and cast back into the fiery chasm from which it came. One of you must do this."

But one council member objects, "One does not simply walk into Mordor. Its black gates are guarded by more than just orcs. There is evil there that does not sleep, and the great eye is ever watchful. It is a barren wasteland, riddled with fire and ash and dust. Not with ten thousand men could you do this. It is folly!"

The council members begin to protest, bicker, and accuse, standing and pointing at each other until a small voice is heard that silences them all. Frodo stands and says, "I will take it. I will take it! I will take the ring to Mordor."

The members of the council are stunned into silence, and one by one they pledge themselves to be a team supporting Frodo. Thus is born "The Fellowship of the Ring."

Frodo, the smallest, least powerful, and humblest of them all, emerges as the greatest because he's willing to do what must be done, regardless of the sacrifice.

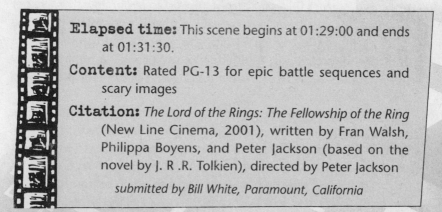

Elapsed time: This scene begins at 01:29:00 and ends at 01:31:30.

Content: Rated PG-13 for epic battle sequences and scary images

Citation: *The Lord of the Rings: The Fellowship of the Ring* (New Line Cinema, 2001), written by Fran Walsh, Philippa Boyens, and Peter Jackson (based on the novel by J. R .R. Tolkien), directed by Peter Jackson

submitted by Bill White, Paramount, California

38. GREED

Gone Nutty

Topic: *The Futility of Greed*

Texts: *Ecclesiastes 5:10; Luke 12:13–21; Philippians 4:11–13; 1 Timothy 6:6–10; Hebrews 13:5–6*

Keywords: *Contentment; Covetousness; Discontent; Evil Desire; Greed; Hunger; Idolatry; Loss; Lusts; Materialism; Money; Sinful Nature; Single-Mindedness; Spiritual Hunger; Unrest*

The animated short *Gone Nutty* opens with Scrat (voiced by Chris Wedge), a neurotic prehistoric squirrel, storing up one last acorn before the Ice Age arrives. From all appearances Scrat has been very busy. As he carries this last acorn to his lair, an old hollow tree, we get a peek at his vast treasure trove of nuts, which completely fills the inner cavity of the tree. Scrat lugs the acorn to the top of the tree and tries to force it into the middle of the pile. It's a tight squeeze, but Scrat pushes the nut down into the center of the acorns. He looks pleased with himself.

As he begins to walk away, though, the nut pops out of place. Scrat calmly returns and pushes it back into place. As he turns to walk away, the nut pops out again. His frustration mounts as he pushes it back down into the hole. After the nut pops out a third time, Scrat becomes more aggressive. He jumps up and down on the acorn, trying to squeeze the stubborn nut into place. Finally the pressure causes the storehouse to explode, sending the acorns and Scrat reeling down an icy incline and off a precipice.

As Scrat free-falls down the deep gorge, he desperately reaches to catch some of the acorns tumbling alongside. He succeeds in grabbing a bunch of acorns, only to slam hard into the canyon's icy floor. As Scrat comes to his senses, he spots an acorn speedily falling toward him. He frantically tries to avoid the impact, but it is to no avail. What's worse, upon impact, the acorn actually triggers an intercontinental divide and leaves a beaten and bruised Scrat on an icy plateau. He reaches down to pull the one remaining acorn out of the ice. When he finally pulls the acorn free, it disintegrates into ashes.

Elapsed time: This short story precedes the movie *Ice Age,* beginning at the opening credit and ending at 00:04:16.

Content: Not rated

Citation: *Gone Nutty* (20th Century Fox, 2002), written by William H. Frake and Dan Shefelman, directed by Carlos Saldanha

submitted by David Slagle, Wilmore, Kentucky

39. HEAVEN

Corrina, Corrina

Topic: *Father Denies Heaven to Grieving Daughter*

Texts: *Ecclesiastes 3:11; John 3:16;
2 Corinthians 4:18; 2 Corinthians 5:1;
1 Thessalonians 4:13; 1 John 5:11–13*

Keywords: *Afterlife; Atheism; Child Rearing; Children;
Death; Doctrine; Eternal Perspective; Grief; Heaven;
Mourning; Orphans; Teachers; Teaching; Worldview*

In the movie *Corrina, Corrina*, jingle writer Manny Singer (played by Ray Liotta) and his young daughter, Molly (played by Tina Majorino), are heartbroken after their loving wife and mother died. They hire a housekeeper, Corrina (played by Whoopi Goldberg), to help them around the house.

In an early scene, deliverymen arrive with furniture ordered by Mrs. Singer prior to her death. When they ask for Mrs. Singer, Mr. Singer says, "She's in the bathtub right now." This sends Molly running anxiously to the bathroom in hopes of finding her mother there.

Later in the movie, Molly is lying in the grass with Corrina next to a dress that belonged to her mother. Corrina says, "You know what I think, Molly? I think your mom is looking down at you from heaven right now. And if you look really close, I'll bet you'll see she's waving."

Manny overhears and pulls Corrina aside. "Corrina, uh, I really appreciate everything you're doing here. And whatever you believe in is fine. Your heaven is fine for you. Molly's mother was an atheist—and so am I—and I don't want you telling her she's somewhere she isn't. Okay?"

Corrina says, "Yes, Mr. Singer. I'll just continue to tell Molly that her mother is in the bathtub!"

Elapsed time: From the New Line Home Video logo, this scene starts at 00:25:27 and ends at 00:27:02.

Content: Rated PG for mature themes

Citation: *Corrina, Corrina* (New Line Cinema, 1994), written and directed by Jessie Nelson

submitted by Van Morris, Mount Washington, Kentucky

40. HELP FROM GOD

The African Queen

Topic: *Divine Intervention*

Texts: *Psalm 63:6–8; Psalm 72:12–14; Psalm 107; 2 Corinthians 12:9–10; 2 Corinthians 13:4*

Keywords: *Deliverance; Dependence on God; Divine Help; God's Providence; Helplessness; Hopelessness; Mercy; Redemption; Salvation; Trials; Weakness*

The African Queen tells the story of Charlie Allnut (played by Humphrey Bogart), a hard drinker who runs a small steamboat, the *African Queen,* through the shallow rivers of East Africa in the early 1900s, bringing dynamite, gin, supplies, and tools to European speculators and miners. He also carries the mail to Rose (played by Katherine Hepburn), a missionary. When World War I breaks out and the Germans burn Rose's home and church, the British missionary and the Canadian boatman flee in the *African Queen.*

Their destination is a large lake downriver, where they hope to assist the Allied war effort by blowing up a German destroyer. On the river they face one danger after another. Insects attack. Bullets whiz by as they pass a German-held fort. They fight rapids. With a lot of moxie they survive these tests, but then the river dissipates and splits into a hundred streams. The *African Queen* bogs down in a marsh.

With no current to push them along, Charlie and Rose use poles to propel forward, and eventually Charlie has to wade the shallows, pulling the boat by a rope. He shudders when he finds leeches on his back and arms, but he grimly returns to the water, and soon Rose herself slogs through the marsh, hacking a path with a machete while Charlie pulls. Eventually they come to the end of their strength. The boat is stuck on a mudflat, and Charlie is feverish.

He says, "Rosie, you want to know the truth, don't you? Even if we had all our strength, we'd never get her off this mud. We're finished."

She responds simply, "I know it," and they resign themselves to death in the wasteland.

As Charlie drifts to sleep, Rose offers a simple prayer of resignation: "We've come to the end of our journey. In a little while we will stand before you. . . . Open the doors of heaven for Charlie and me."

But the camera slowly draws back to reveal what the couple cannot see because of the reeds—the *African Queen* is less than a hundred yards from the shining lake. The camera then transports us far upstream to the river's headwaters. A torrential rainstorm is sending animals scurrying for cover. Further downstream, the rains have turned the rapids into cataracts. Down on the mudflat a small channel begins to run through the reeds. The channel swells, gently lifts the *Queen* off the mudflat, and carries it to the lake. Charlie and Rose awaken to the gentle rocking of the boat and a refreshing breeze.

Reaching the end of human resources can mark the beginning of divine intervention.

Elapsed time: Measured from the beginning of the opening credit, this scene begins at 01:19:00 and ends at 01:25:00.

Content: Not rated

Citation: *The African Queen* (20th Century Fox, 1951), written by James Agee (based on the novel by C. S. Forester), directed by John Huston

submitted by Jeff Arthurs, South Hamilton, Massachusetts

41. HEROES

Eight Men Out

Topic: *When Heroes Disappoint*

Texts: *Matthew 5:13–16; 1 Corinthians 10:6–13; 2 Corinthians 8:21; 1 Timothy 3:1–15; 1 Timothy 4:16; 1 Timothy 5:19–25; 2 Timothy 2:20–22; Titus 1:5–9; James 3:1*

Keywords: *Church Leaders; Example; Gambling; Heroes; Integrity; Leadership; Pastors*

Eight Men Out is the historical drama about the infamous Chicago White Sox scandal of 1919. When many of the players felt cheated and demoralized by owner Charles Comiskey's penny-pinching and tough-handed ways, gamblers influenced several of them to lose the World Series in exchange for a large amount of money. A newspaper reporter exposed the scandal. A sympathetic jury later found them not guilty, but the commissioner of baseball banned them from the major leagues for life.

Players Shoeless Joe Jackson and Happy Felsch have different reactions when their corruption is exposed. In one scene, Shoeless Joe (played by D. B. Sweeney) is sitting uncomfortably in front of several grand jury lawyers with a form in front of him. The lawyers tell him they're after the gamblers, not the ballplayers, and they want him to sign to be a witness. After a moment's hesitation he reluctantly puts an "X" on the line, puts down the pen, and looks away in embarrassment and defeat.

In another scene, Happy Felsch (played by Charlie Sheen) is drinking beer with several friends in a bar. One of them says, "The word is, you made a bundle."

Felsch replies, "Sure, I saw some cash. They promised us twenty grand each, but all I saw was five. What am I gonna do, call a cop?" Everyone laughs.

Another man asks him, "So why did you do it? Somebody lean on you?"

Felsch replies matter-of-factly, "Everybody else was getting some. I figured without the pitchers we were going to lose anyway, so why shouldn't I get fat, too? I may be dumb, fellows, but I'm not stupid." Everyone laughs.

In the next scene Shoeless Joe is walking out of the meeting room with a lawyer, who asks, "Now that wasn't so bad, was it, Joe?"

Joe answers, "It kind of felt good to get it off my chest."

"You did the right thing, Joe. We're proud of you."

They open a large door leading to the street and are immediately met by reporters and flashing cameras. As Joe makes his way through the crowd, various questions are asked: "Hey, what do you say, Joe? Were you in on it? Who did all the brain work? Why did you wait so long to spill it, Joe?" He gives a brief answer.

Then a little boy's voice is clearly heard: "Joe!" Everyone stops. Joe turns to look at the boy, who is about ten years old. In an innocent, pleading voice, the boy says, "Say it ain't so, Joe. Say it ain't so."

Joe looks down, says nothing, then continues walking. The roar of the reporters recommences as they follow him, leaving the boy standing alone, staring after them.

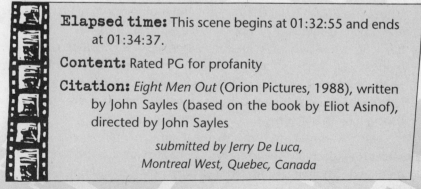

Elapsed time: This scene begins at 01:32:55 and ends at 01:34:37.

Content: Rated PG for profanity

Citation: *Eight Men Out* (Orion Pictures, 1988), written by John Sayles (based on the book by Eliot Asinof), directed by John Sayles

submitted by Jerry De Luca,
Montreal West, Quebec, Canada

42. HONOR

A Beautiful Mind

Topic: Honored by Peers

Texts: Acts 20:24; 1 Corinthians 9:24–27; Hebrews 12:1

Keywords: Adversity; Encouragement; Eternal Life; Honor; Perseverance; Recognition; Rewards

A *Beautiful Mind* tells the story of John Nash (played by Russell Crowe), a brilliant mathematician whose career and life were crippled by schizophrenia. Nash taught at M.I.T. until schizophrenia and delusions took over his life. After years of struggle, he began teaching at Princeton and went on to win the Nobel Prize for his theory of the dynamics of human conflict as it relates to economics.

Toward the end of the movie, Nash is invited into the professors' lounge by a man who has just told him he's being considered for the Nobel Prize. Nash is uncertain of how he should respond; he wonders if his mind is fabricating a dream. He even asks a student whether the man is real or a hallucination. When Nash is convinced that the man and his invitation are genuine, he still resists, feeling unworthy of the exclusivity of the professors' lounge. He never enters this lounge, aware that his episodes of psychotic behavior are known all too well by the faculty.

Nash walks warily through the Gothic entrance and sits at a table. Unexpectedly, the professors begin to walk over to John's table and lay down their pens in front of him. This is a tradition Princeton faculty use to honor highly esteemed colleagues. One by one, the professors acknowledge their love and support for the troubled man who, despite difficulties, stayed the course: "It's an honor, John." "It's a privilege, John." "Congratulations, John."

Elapsed time: Measured from the beginning of the opening credit, this scene begins at 01:59:57 and ends at 02:04:43.

Content: Rated PG-13 for profanity, sexuality, and violence

Citation: *A Beautiful Mind* (Universal Pictures, 2001), written by Akiva Goldsman (based on the book by Sylvia Nasar), directed by Ron Howard

submitted by David Slagle, Wilmore, Kentucky

43. HUMAN HELP

One True Thing

Topic: *Cancer Patient Helps Needy Friend*

Texts: *Luke 10:25–37; John 15:12–17;*
Galatians 5:13–14; Philippians 2:1–4;
1 Thessalonians 4:9–10

Keywords: *Caring; Compassion; Convenience; Disease;*
Dying to Self; Human Help; Kindness; Love; Ministry;
Overcoming; Selflessness; Unselfishness; Weakness

One True Thing is about a courageous housewife, Kate (played by Meryl Streep), who is dying of cancer.

At the onset of her illness, Kate is often well enough to drive a car. In one scene Kate is driving with her friend Clarice (played by Mary Catherine Wright) next to her, and her daughter, Ellen (played by Renee Zellweger), in the backseat. Kate and Clarice are enjoying themselves, singing loudly and off-key to some song on the radio, while Ellen squirms uncomfortably, wishing she were somewhere else.

Ellen asks when they'll be turning around and heading home. When Kate tells her they still need to buy some yarn, Ellen resigns herself to boredom.

Later as Clarice is getting out of the car, thanking Kate profusely, she tells Ellen, "I love your mother!"

Ellen gets into the front seat, and they drive off. Kate asks her daughter, "Well, I think she had fun, don't you?" She asks for a pill from the glove compartment and takes it. Ellen answers her with a calm but impatient tone. "No idea. We've been driving around for hours, wasting time. You don't feel well, and I need to meet Dad."

Kate responds with calmness and conviction. "We just dropped Clarice off at her mother's house. That's because she's been living there four months since her husband left her and she hit rock bottom." This gets Ellen's attention, and she looks at her mother. "And she stays inside all day. Shades drawn. Every day. So one of us comes up once a week and takes her out. You know, have some fun. Have some laughs. And that's what we did today. I hope."

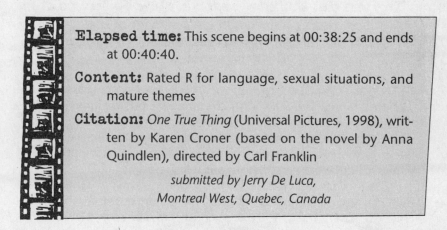

Elapsed time: This scene begins at 00:38:25 and ends at 00:40:40.

Content: Rated R for language, sexual situations, and mature themes

Citation: *One True Thing* (Universal Pictures, 1998), written by Karen Croner (based on the novel by Anna Quindlen), directed by Carl Franklin

submitted by Jerry De Luca,
Montreal West, Quebec, Canada

44. HUMAN WORTH

A.I.

Topic: *The Worth of All Humans*

Texts: *Genesis 1:26–27; Psalm 139:13–16; Matthew 6:26*

Keywords: *Brotherly Love; Christ's Love; Fatherhood of God; God's Love; Human Worth; Image of God; Love; Meaning of Life; Prejudice; Racism*

The Steven Spielberg movie *A.I.: Artificial Intelligence* (based on the late Stanley Kubrick's long-cherished vision) critiques the tendency of our culture toward dehumanization. In the film, robots, which represent life, are disposed of when they are perceived as useless or undesirable. The film paints a disturbing picture of a world where others are used to satisfy our selfish desires.

Charles Colson writes about the movie in *BreakPoint* magazine*:

"The story develops around David—a sort of cybernetic Pinocchio. Created in the image of a scientist's own lost son, David ushers in a new technological era. Like other androids, he can think, but unlike other mechanical beings, David can also feel. David can feel more than the sensation of pain or cold, but he was programmed with the ability to bond, trust, love, and hate.

"David is given to a couple whose own son is comatose and whose recovery was beyond the reach of science. The mother is distraught at the loss of her child. When her husband brings David home, she at first resists. But . . . she decides to initiate the program to make David love her. They enjoy a short time of bonding as mother and son until her real flesh-and-blood son amazingly recovers.

"When the couple's son returns from the hospital, David finds that his mother no longer loves him because he is not real. Like Pinocchio, he sets out to become a real boy—in the hope that his mother will then love him.

"During David's search to become a real boy he meets another android, Joe. Joe says to David that love is given only when something can be gotten in return. He tells David that his mother didn't love him and never would:

DAVID: My mommy doesn't hate me, because I'm special and unique. Because there's never been anyone like me before—ever.... I am real. Mommy is going to read to me and tuck me in my bed and sing to me and listen to what I say, and she will cuddle me and tell me a hundred times a day that she loves me.

JOE: She loves what you do for her.... She does not love you, David. She cannot love you. You are neither flesh nor blood. You were designed and built specific like the rest of us. And you are alone now only because they are tired of you or replaced you with a younger model or were displeased with something you said or broke.

"In contrast to much of the world, the message of Scripture is that human dignity doesn't come from usefulness. Dignity does not come from a person's religion, nor their sex, nor from their skin color, nor age, nor because of their power or status. Human dignity is something we are conceived with because we are made in the image of God. A quadriplegic has the same dignity as an Olympic athlete; a Muslim the same dignity as a Christian; a Samaritan the same dignity as a Jew. These are our neighbors whom we are to love as ourselves."

Elapsed time: Measured from the beginning of the opening credit, this scene begins at 01:30:27 and lasts about forty-five seconds.

Content: Rated PG-13 for profanity and sexual situations

Citation: *A.I.* (Warner Brothers, 2001), written by Steven Spielberg and Ian Watson (based on the short story "Supertoys Last All Summer Long" by Brian Aldiss), directed by Steven Spielberg

*Charles Colson, "A Little Too Close to Home," BreakPoint (15 August 2001). Copyright © 2001 by Prison Fellowship. Used by permission.

submitted by Aaron Goerner, Utica, New York

45. IMAGE OF GOD

The Wizard of Oz

Topic: *Wrong Idea of Majesty*

Texts: *Exodus 19; Psalm 136:3–26; John 3:16; Ephesians 2:3–7; Hebrews 12:14–29; Revelation 4; Revelation 5*

Keywords: *Experiencing God; Fear of God; God's Attributes; God's Holiness; God's Love; God's Majesty; God's Power; Image of God; Knowing God; Reverence*

In *The Wizard of Oz,* Dorothy, the Lion, the Scarecrow, and the Tin Man arrive at the legendary Emerald City to meet with the Wizard (played by Frank Morgan). The Wizard is reputed to hold the power to solve each of the travelers' problems. But to enter his presence, they must first traverse a long, dimly lit Gothic hallway. The Lion is not alone in his cowardice as they enter the large inner sanctum. They are greeted with an explosion and billows of green smoke.

When the smoke finally clears, a giant, menacing, bodiless head shouts, "I am Oz, the great and terrible! Who are you?"

Dorothy (played by Judy Garland) attempts a response, but the Wizard booms, "Silence! The great and powerful Oz knows why you are here! Step forward, Tin Man."

The Tin Man (played by Jack Haley) approaches this ominous-looking figure with great trepidation, only to hear the Wizard say, "You dare come to me for a heart, you clinking, clanking, clattering collection of caliginous junk?"

The other travelers are met with similar greetings. To the Scarecrow (played by Ray Bolger), the Wizard shouts, "You have the effrontery to ask for a brain, you billowing bale of bovine fodder?" To the Cowardly Lion (played by Bert Lahr), he shouts, "And you, Lion?" The poor Lion is overcome with fear and faints.

Sadly, this is similar to the unflattering caricature summoned up by many when they think about God. The Wizard puts on a false show of majesty, but there is no love, no grace, no mercy.

In several places, the Scriptures paint an awesome picture of the holiness of God and the reverence he rightly inspires. At Mount Sinai, as well as in visions given to Isaiah and Ezekiel, God manifests himself with fire and smoke and authority. That is who God is. But God is also loving and compassionate and gentle. We must hold both views of God in balance.

Elapsed time: Measured from the MGM logo, this scene begins at 01:09:43 and ends at about 01:12:43.

Content: Rated G

Citation: *The Wizard of Oz* (MGM, 1939), written by Noel Langley, Florence Ryerson, and Edgar Allan Woolf (based on the novel by L. Frank Baum), directed by Victor Fleming

submitted by David Slagle, Wilmore, Kentucky

46. INHERITANCE

Uncorked

Topic: The Gift You Cannot Earn

Texts: Matthew 6:33; Luke 15:31; Romans 8:31–33; Ephesians 2:8–9

Keywords: Eternal Life; Grace; Inheritance; Possessions; Salvation as Gift; Self-Centeredness

Uncorked is about an ambitious, self-absorbed man's futile search for wealth. Ross (played by Rufus Sewell) is determined to sell a priceless family wine collection in order to buy a local manganese mine, which he hopes will earn him great wealth. His eccentric Uncle Cullen (played by Nigel Hawthorne) is unimpressed by his nephew's materialism.

Ross broods over how to get his brother and uncle to sign over the estate to him. When this fails, he inveigles his girlfriend in an unseemly plan to murder his Uncle Cullen. But in his moment of madness he restrains himself and is remorseful about his self-centeredness. While he apologizes to his uncle, he indicates he'll be finding a place of his own.

Cullen acknowledges his nephew's contrition and smiles. "Well, let me tell you something," Cullen says. "You already have a place of your own. You already own Sachem Farm."

Unwilling to believe what he heard, Ross runs to the family safe. Upon opening it he discovers that the deed to the estate has had his name on it all along. Ross wonders aloud if this all could be true.

Cullen calls attention to a blue folder also in the safe. His nephew looks into the folder and pulls out a key. With a flash of insight, Ross runs to the entrance to the mine. The key fits the lock. Amazingly, the mine he longed to own was already in the family. It was a birthright he could only accept as a gift, not earn or buy.

Elapsed time: Measured from the beginning of the opening credit, this scene begins at 01:20:45 and ends at 01:22:45.

Content: Rated PG for language

Citation: *Uncorked* (Trimark, 2001; previously released as *At Sachem Farm*, 1998), written and directed by John Huddles

submitted by Greg Asimakoupoulos, Naperville, Illinois

47. INJUSTICE

The Green Mile

Topic: *Suffering Injustice*

Texts: *Psalm 22:1–14; Matthew 5:38–42; Luke 23:14–24; 1 Peter 2:19–25*

Keywords: *Christ's Cross; Injustice; Self-Sacrifice*

The Green Mile is set in the South in 1935. Paul Edgecomb (played by Tom Hanks) is head guard of death row in a Louisiana prison. It is called "the green mile" because of the long, lime-colored floor prisoners must walk to get to the electric chair.

Paul develops a special relationship with John Coffey (played by Michael Clarke Duncan), a slightly retarded, seven-foot black man who has been falsely charged with the murder of two white girls.

Paul soon discovers that John possesses a mysterious gift—a gift John calls "taking it back." He can absorb another's disease or death, rendering them cured.

Although John is able to convince Paul that he found the girls already dead (and had tried to revive them prior to being apprehended), Paul is unable to stay John's execution.

As the scene opens, Paul is reading the court record of what happened the day John Coffey was arrested. A farmer's wife is on the telephone pleading for help. She has just discovered that her two school-age girls have been kidnapped from their bedroom. As she frantically speaks to the operator, her husband and son race out to look for the girls. As word of the kidnapping reaches neighboring farmers, they join the father in a massive search party.

Suddenly a bloodcurdling scream is heard. After slogging through a swamp in the direction of the scream, the farmer and his friends come upon a gigantic black man cradling the lifeless bodies of the two sisters. He is sobbing uncontrollably. "I couldn't help it! I tried to take it back, but it was too late," he cries.

The sheriff pulls the incensed father away from the presumed killer and says, "You are under arrest for murder," before spitting in John's face. But the gentle giant does not fight back.

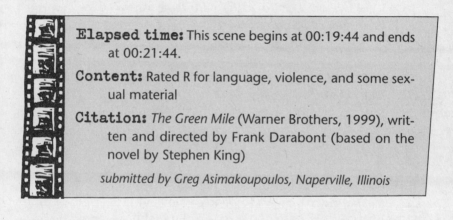

Elapsed time: This scene begins at 00:19:44 and ends at 00:21:44.

Content: Rated R for language, violence, and some sexual material

Citation: *The Green Mile* (Warner Brothers, 1999), written and directed by Frank Darabont (based on the novel by Stephen King)

submitted by Greg Asimakoupoulos, Naperville, Illinois

48. JUDGMENT

Flatliners

Topic: *Haunted by Past Sins*

Texts: *Psalm 32:3–5; Psalm 51:3; Psalm 139:7–23; Luke 22:60–62; Romans 14:10–12; 2 Corinthians 5:10; Hebrews 9:27*

Keywords: *Conscience; Death; Guilt; Judgment; Past; Regret; Responsibility; Sin*

Flatliners is about five medical students in Chicago who are curious about what occurs to people who flatline (ceasing of heart and brain activity) and then are resuscitated. These would-be doctors decide to induce their own near-death experiences by ingesting an anesthetic and stopping their heart with electrical paddles.

Sneaking into a vacant building to keep this illegal activity from being discovered, they take turns "flatlining." After each is technically dead for three or four minutes, the others attempt to bring him or her back. In the process of "dying" and returning, each student is sensitized to the unconfessed sins of the past. In each case they describe the nightmarish visions they had while unconscious, convincing them that the afterlife is not a figment of the imagination.

In Nelson's (played by Kiefer Sutherland) brush with death, he traveled back twenty years to a meadow where he and his dog chased a boy up a tree and taunted him. The limb broke, and the child fell to his death.

Having relived the tragedy, Nelson is somber as he walks aimlessly in downtown Chicago in the rainy predawn darkness. Nelson's mind plays tricks on him. His guilt causes what is real and what is imaginary to blur.

The sound of cyclists riding by startles him like a swarm of bees. He walks into a dark alley and sees faces of street people who look up at him with searing glances. One of them is a homeless woman who is warming herself by a fire and talking to herself. Her words are disconnected and don't make sense. But when Nelson walks past her, she looks directly at him and mysteriously calls him by name. Then, with obvious sarcasm, she speaks words he already feels in his heart: "'Cause in the end we all know what we've done."

This stranger's uninvited promise of judgment frightens Nelson, and he runs away into the darkness.

Elapsed time: This scene begins at 00:39:00 and ends at about 00:40:30.

Content: Rated R for sexual situations and language

Citation: *Flatliners* (Columbia Pictures, 1990), written by Peter Filardi, directed by Joel Schumacher

submitted by Greg Asimakoupoulos, Naperville, Illinois

49. LEADERSHIP

To Kill a Mockingbird

Topic: *Father Honored*

Texts: *Matthew 23:12; Romans 13:7; Ephesians 6:2; Philippians 2:29; 1 Timothy 5:17*

Keywords: *Honor; Humility; Injustice; Justice; Leadership; Respect*

The 1962 film *To Kill a Mockingbird* stars Gregory Peck as Atticus Finch, a lawyer living in Macon, Georgia, during the 1940s. Atticus is a widower raising two children while operating his own law practice. He defends a local black man, Tom Robinson, who is accused of raping a local young white lady. The lawyer mounts a noble defense—one that leaves one highly doubtful of the defendant's guilt. However, most of the townspeople are not convinced. The father of the woman who was allegedly raped is outraged that Atticus would defend a black man.

After being tipped off that a mob is going to break into the jail and take the prisoner, Atticus sits outside the jail, guarding his client. Carloads of angry men arrive, some carrying rifles, and threaten Atticus, demanding that he step aside. He stands firm.

After an emotional trial in which the accuser insists that the defendant is guilty and the accused tearfully proclaims his innocence, the all-white jury files back into the courtroom. Deliberations have concluded, and a cloud of quiet anticipation settles over the segregated courtroom.

The judge asks, "Gentlemen of the jury, have you reached a verdict?" The jurors reply, "Guilty." At first Atticus's eyes reveal shock and disbelief. He then gathers himself and directs his concern toward his client, pleading with him to remain hopeful and patient, while vowing to appeal. (Sadly, there is no need for an appeal, because later that evening the sheriff notifies Atticus that, while being transferred, Robinson made a run for it and was shot and killed.)

As the courtroom clears and Atticus collects his papers, one by one the black townspeople seated in the balcony with Atticus's two children stand out of respect. A black minister says to Atticus's daughter, "Miss Jean Louise. Miss Jean Louise. Stand up. Your father's passing by."

Jean Louise stands, and Atticus leaves the courtroom, his head hung low, appearing not to even see the honor being shown to him.

Elapsed time: Measured from the beginning of the opening credit, this scene begins at 01:40:38 and ends at 01:43:08.

Content: Not rated

Citation: *To Kill a Mockingbird* (Universal Pictures, 1962), written by Horton Foote (based on the novel by Harper Lee), directed by Robert Mulligan

submitted by Van Morris, Mount Washington, Kentucky

50. LOVE

A Beautiful Mind

Topic: *Loving the Unlovable*

Texts: *John 3:16; Romans 5:8; 1 Corinthians 13; Ephesians 5:1–2; Colossians 3:12–14; 1 John 3:1–3*

Keywords: *Christ's Cross; Christ's Love; Devotion; Difficulties; Divorce; God's Love; Illness; Love; Marriage; Overcoming; Perseverance; Relationships; Romantic Love; Sacrifice*

A *Beautiful Mind* tells the story of John Nash (played by Russell Crowe), a brilliant mathematician whose career and life were crippled by schizophrenia. Nash taught at M.I.T. and went on to win the Nobel Prize for his theory of the dynamics of human conflict as it relates to economics.

In anticipation of the airing of "A Brilliant Madness: The True Story of John Nash" on WLRN Public Television, an April 8, 2002, news release summarized Nash's story: "At the height of his career, after a decade of remarkable mathematical accomplishments, Nash suffered a breakdown. . . . His wife, Alicia, had him committed against his will to a private mental hospital, where he was diagnosed with paranoid schizophrenia and treated with psychoanalysis. Upon his release, Nash abruptly resigned from M.I.T., withdrew his pension fund, and fled to Europe. . . . He saw himself as a secret messenger of God and the focus of an international communist conspiracy. With help from the State Department, Alicia had him deported back to the United

States. Desperate and short of funds, Alicia was forced to commit her husband to the former New Jersey Lunatic Asylum, an understaffed state institution."

In one scene from *A Beautiful Mind,* one of John's colleagues is talking to Alicia (played by Jennifer Connelly). "So, Alicia, how are you holding up?"

Alicia responds feebly, "Well, the delusions have passed. They're saying with medications . . ."

The colleague clarifies, "No, I mean you."

Alicia pauses and explains, "I think often what I feel is obligation, or guilt, over wanting to leave, rage against John, against God. But then I look at him, and I force myself to see the man that I married, and he becomes that man. He's transformed into someone that I love, and I'm transformed into someone that loves him. It's not all the time, but it's enough."

"I think John is a very lucky man," the colleague says.

In the movie, Nash's wife sticks by him through thick and thin. In real life, it wasn't that easy. Alicia eventually divorced him. Later, though, they reconciled. Both the movie and the real story affirm the difficulty—and beauty—of loving those who are hard to love. We wonder at the possibility that someone could love a person who is difficult or unlovely, and then we are jolted back to the reality of Christ's cross, where we see the epitome of the beautiful mind—the beautiful mind of a holy, just, and merciful God condescending to love a race of undeserving sinners.

Elapsed time: Measured from the beginning of the opening credit, this scene begins at 01:20:18 and ends at 01:22:06.

Content: Rated PG-13 for profanity, sexuality, and violence

Citation: *A Beautiful Mind* (Universal Pictures, 2001), written by Akiva Goldsman (based on the book by Sylvia Nasar), directed by Ron Howard

submitted by David Slagle, Wilmore, Kentucky

51. MANIPULATION

Waking Ned Devine

Topic: *Husband Manipulates Wife for an Apple Tart*

Texts: *John 13:1–17; Galatians 5:13*

Keywords: *Deception; Gambling; Laziness; Lying; Manipulation; Marriage; Motivation; Servanthood*

Waking Ned Devine begins in the cozy living room of an elderly Irish couple. In the background we hear a television announcer informing the audience that the big jackpot lottery numbers are about to be announced. The husband, Jackie (played by Ian Bannen), settles into a comfortable brown chair in front of the television set. We can see his wife in the background, doing paperwork in the kitchen. Once Jackie is happily ensconced in his old brown chair, anticipating the announcement of the lottery numbers, he calls out to Annie, his wife (played by Fionnula Flanagan), "Honey, where's me ticket?"

"It's in your trousers," she says.

"Annie, bring me me apple tart, will you."

"Get it yourself," responds Annie.

"Annie, the lottery started," he says. "Oh, yes, there she goes, number 19. Annie, come in. Bring me me tart. We got the first one." Jackie appears very pleased he has the first of six lottery numbers, but Annie seems unimpressed and still makes no move to bring Jackie his apple tart.

"Jeepers, Annie. Can you believe it, I got the second," says Jackie as he sits a little straighter in his seat.

The television announcer gives the third number. Jackie checks his ticket and says, "Oh, will you look at that, girl!" Annie is still ignoring him.

A fourth number is announced, and Jackie yells out, "I can't believe it, Annie. I got the first four!"

Now Annie pays attention. She gets up, apple tart in hand, and starts into the room. She is visibly stunned. She puts the apple tart into Jackie's hands.

Jackie begins to eat the apple tart and says, "Annie, we've got it!"

"Jackie, that's five," says a slack-jawed Annie.

"God help us, God help us," says Jackie as the television announcer begins to announce the sixth and final number. The room is thick with anticipation, and Jackie continues to consume his apple tart.

"Now here's the sixth number," says the announcer.

When he calls out the number, Jackie yells, "Yes! Yes! Yes! Yes! Yes! Yes! Yes!" All the while he is laughing maniacally and tearing up the lottery ticket.

A confused Annie asks, "Have we won?"

A wily Jackie responds, "No, but it got me apple tart brought in, didn't it."

Elapsed time: Measured from the Fox logo, this scene begins at 00:01:33 and ends at 00:03:42.

Content: Rated PG for nudity and mature themes

Citation: *Waking Ned Devine* (Fox Searchlight Pictures, 1998), written and directed by Kirk Jones

submitted by David Slagle, Wilmore, Kentucky

52. MARRIAGE

A Doll's House

Topic: *Feminist Notions Ruin Marriage*

Texts: *Proverbs 31:10–12; Ephesians 5:22–24; 2 Timothy 3:2; James 3:14–16; 1 Peter 3:1–6*

Keywords: *Duty; Feminism; Freedom; Husbands; Love; Marriage; Mothers; Parenting; Responsibility; Selfishness; Vocation; Vows; Wives; Women*

Set in nineteenth-century Norway, *A Doll's House* is the story of a young housewife and mother (played by Jane Fonda) who lies to her husband and forges a document to gain money for a good cause. The lie is eventually exposed and the problems resolved, but Nora comes to believe that leaving her family will bring her true freedom.

Near the film's end, Nora sits in the living room of a lavish home with her husband, Torvald (played by David Warner). Nora tells her husband, "We've been married eight years. This is the first time that you and I, man and wife, have ever had a serious talk together."

Torvald tells her that he never wanted her to take on his worries. Nora explains that growing up she only adopted her father's opinions, and then married Torvald.

He asks her, "Have you never been happy here?"

Nora thinks to herself for a moment and replies, "I always thought I was, but I haven't ever been. No. I've had fun. You've always been very kind to me, Torvald, but this house has been like a playroom. My children have been my dolls."

"So, playing is over. We'll begin again. Now comes the time to learn," Torvald pleads. But Nora disagrees, explaining that Torvald couldn't teach her to be the right wife for him and that she isn't fit to educate her children.

She explains, "I have to educate myself first. And you can't do that for me. That is something that I must do for myself. That is why I'm leaving you."

Shocked, Torvald continues to listen to Nora's plans to return to her hometown. She has no working experience but must try to get some. Torvald strides toward her and argues, "You forget your most sacred duty. Your husband. Your children. Your position as mother and wife."

"I have another duty, equally 'sacred,' if that is the word. My duty to myself," she snaps.

Torvald exclaims, "You're first and foremost a wife and mother!"

"I can't believe that anymore," Nora explains. "I believe that first and foremost I am a human being like you. Or I must become one."

Torvald asks her about her sense of duty. Nora responds that these things have different meanings. She doesn't believe that certain accepted laws are right.

Torvald quietly states, "You don't love me."

Plainly, Nora utters, "No. That's exactly it. I can't help it. I don't love you anymore."

Elapsed time: Measured from the beginning of the opening credit, this scene begins at 01:39:05 and ends at 01:41:52.

Content: Rated G

Citation: *A Doll's House* (World Film Services, 1973), written by David Mercer (based on the play by Henrik Ibsen), directed by Joseph Losey

submitted by Jerry De Luca,
Montreal West, Quebec, Canada

53. MARRIAGE

The Odd Couple II

Topic: *Fear of Commitment*

Texts: *Deuteronomy 30:15–20; Joshua 24:15; Psalm 45:10–17; Song of Songs 2:8–13; Matthew 22:36–38*

Keywords: *Choices; Commitment; Decisions; Fear; Love; Marriage; Romance; Uncertainties*

In *The Odd Couple II*, Oscar Madison's son, Brucey, is getting married. The ceremony and reception are about to begin in Oscar's large, luxurious house. Oscar (played by Walter Matthau) discovers his son (played by Jonathan Silverman) has contracted cold feet and is sitting outside alone—on the roof.

At the start of this scene, Oscar enters an upstairs bedroom, walks to the window, and greets his son, who is sitting just outside on the peak of the roof. His son looks worried and discouraged.

"I hope you don't think I'm meddling," Oscar says, "but were you planning on coming to the wedding today?"

Brucey answers, "I was thinking about it."

"You're nervous, huh?" Oscar asks.

"I was thinking I'd be making a big mistake," Brucey says. "I don't trust marriage. I mean, look at everyone here. Look at my own family. Mom was married three times. You were married one time, and then never again for thirty years. Hers were too many. Yours were not enough. So tell me, what is wrong with it that frightens everyone so much?"

"I don't know, Brucey. It's like baseball. Either you can play or you can't play. Your mother could play. I couldn't play. Trouble with your mother was she kept getting traded all the time."

"That was not the answer I was looking for," Brucey says.

"Then why did you wait so long to ask the question?" asks his dad.

"Because it's what I thought I wanted. Now I know that it's not what I want."

"Then get out of it," advises his dad. "Don't do it, Brucey. Let me go talk to the others. I'll figure something out to say."

Oscar walks away from the window and is about to exit the bedroom door. But Oscar's quick agreement surprises Brucey. So Brucey comes down from the roof and steps through the window. He tells Oscar that he really does love her. Oscar insists that Brucey will have "two years of excitement and forty-five years of hell."

Brucey insists that marriage is right for him, even if it didn't work for his father. He tells Oscar he is going ahead with the wedding—and he does.

Elapsed time: This scene begins at 01:16:18 and ends at 01:18:22. Caution: End clip right after "You go tell everybody I'm getting dressed." A vulgar word is spoken a few seconds later.

Content: Rated PG-13 for profanity and mature themes

Citation: *The Odd Couple II* (Paramount Pictures, 1998), written by Neil Simon, directed by Howard Deutch

submitted by Jerry De Luca,
Montreal West, Quebec, Canada

54. MATERIALISM

VeggieTales: Madame Blueberry

Topic: *Wanting More Stuff*

Texts: *Proverbs 14:30; Proverbs 23:17; Philippians 4:10–19; Colossians 3:5–6; Hebrews 13:5–6*

Keywords: *Contentment; Coveting; Covetousness; Discontent; Envy; Greed; Materialism; Possessions*

This VeggieTales "lesson in thankfulness" tells the story of Madame Blueberry, a very depressed blueberry who resides in a tree house. She is not content with anything she owns: her dishes are chipped, the knives are too dull, the spoons are too small. Madame Blueberry sings a mournful ditty about her neighbors, who all have more wonderful things than she.

She sings to her butlers, Larry the Cucumber and Bob the Tomato: "I'm so blue, blue, blue, blue. I'm so blue I don't know what to do. My friends all have nice things. I've seen them myself. In fact, I keep pictures up here on my shelf!"

Framed pictures of her neighbors' belongings line her shelf. There are pictures of one neighbor's Crock-Pot, one neighbor's flatware, and another neighbor's ceramic jars with all kinds of sauces. Although her two-story tree house appears to be attractive and well furnished, Madame Blueberry is hopelessly dissatisfied.

One day a new megastore called Stuff-Mart moves across the street. The sign glitters like a beacon of hope to Madame Blueberry.

She has only just seen the sign when three "helpful representatives" from Stuff-Mart show up at her door to confirm her suspicions that her stuff is outdated and that she needs some more.

These dapper sales-vegetables tell her about Stuff-Mart's remarkable line of stuff: refrigerators that store extra mashed potatoes, giant air compressors that blow fruit flies off your dresser, and solar turkey choppers. They sing, "Happiness waits at the Stuff-Mart. All you need is lots more stuff!"

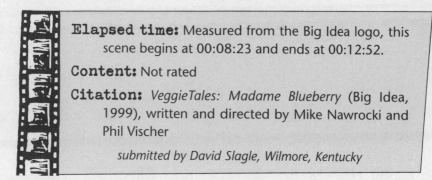

Elapsed time: Measured from the Big Idea logo, this scene begins at 00:08:23 and ends at 00:12:52.

Content: Not rated

Citation: *VeggieTales: Madame Blueberry* (Big Idea, 1999), written and directed by Mike Nawrocki and Phil Vischer

submitted by David Slagle, Wilmore, Kentucky

55. MORALITY

Changing Lanes

Topic: *Moral Relativism in Business*

Texts: *Matthew 5:8; Acts 5:1–11; Romans 2:14–15; 2 Timothy 2:22; James 5:4–5*

Keywords: *Ambition; Business; Career; Conscience; Convictions; Dishonesty; Guilt; Integrity; Money; Morality; Righteousness; Uprightness; Work*

In *Changing Lanes* Ben Affleck plays a young Wall Street lawyer named Gavin Banek. The movie begins with Gavin speeding to the courthouse to file papers that will give his firm power to control the assets of the deceased Mr. Dunne's charitable foundation. Unconvinced of the legitimacy of his firm's case, he repeatedly tells himself, "I did absolutely nothing wrong." On his way to court, he gets in a car accident, and he accidentally leaves behind the file that contains the power of attorney papers signed by Mr. Dunne. Without this file, his firm's case for controlling Mr. Dunne's assets is null and void.

As the movie progresses, Gavin comes to the realization that he had taken advantage of Mr. Dunne. Though his partners assured him there was nothing wrong with getting the feeble old man to sign the power of attorney over to them, Gavin soon realizes it was extortion. As he plans to confess this to the judge, his senior partners forge new documents to replace the lost ones and file them with the court.

After hours, when the other employees have gone home, Gavin goes to one of his partners to discuss his plans, at which time his senior partner (Gavin's father-in-law, played by Sydney Pollack) tells him it's taken care of. Aware that Gavin's conscience is getting in the way, the partner begins to rationalize his actions and explain why he is no worse than Mr. Dunne himself.

"You think those factories in Malaysia have day care centers?" the senior partner asks about Mr. Dunne's business. "Want to check the pollution levels of his chemical plants in Mexico, or look at the tax benefits he got from his foundation?"

"This is all a tightrope. You gotta learn to balance," he advises Gavin.

"How can you live like that?" Gavin asks.

The senior partner answers, "I can live with myself because at the end of the day I think I do more good than harm. What other standard have I got to judge by?"

Elapsed time: Measured from the beginning of the opening credit, this scene begins at 01:23:25 and ends at 01:24:12.

Content: Rated R for language

Citation: *Changing Lanes* (Paramount Pictures, 2002), written by Chap Taylor and Michael Tolkin, directed by Roger Michell

submitted by Debi Zahn, Stratford, Iowa

56. MOTIVATION

Monsters, Inc.

Topic: *Living on the Right Kind of Fuel*

Texts: *Nehemiah 8:10; Philippians 4:4; 1 Peter 3:14*

Keywords: *Anger; Fear; Happiness; Humor; Joy; Laughter; Love; Motivation; Motives; Worry*

Monsters, Inc. is about a monster world that is fueled by fear—literally. The company motto is "We scare because we care." Each day, Mike, Sully, and the other monsters line up on the shop floor as a machine carries dozens of closet doors to individual scaring stations. A scream collection canister rests alongside each closet door, which is a portal to the room of a small child. If the monster does his job correctly, he will elicit a scream from the child that will be sucked into the scream canister and, *voila,* be converted to power.

Mike and Sully are the number one scare team. Sully (voiced by John Goodman), an easygoing, large, blue, fluffy creature, is the primary scarer. Mike (voiced by Billy Crystal), his assistant, is an impatient green Cyclops, 90 percent eyeball and 10 percent arms and legs.

By the end of the movie, the scream-collection business is not going well, and the company is scheduled to shut down. Mike and Sully lament the closing of the company as they depart Monsters, Inc. for what appears to be the last time. Mike responds, "Yeah, but we had a lot of laughs."

We see an idea crossing Sully's face. "Laughs," he says thoughtfully.

In the next scene, the closet door of a child's room opens and an ominous shadow falls across the frightened child and his bed. The light comes on and we see Mike, who pulls out a stool and begins a comedy routine. "Hey, it's great to be in your room! You're in kindergarten, right? Hey, I loved kindergarten. Best three years of my life!" The jokes are so bad that Mike has to resort to lowbrow burping humor, but the results are magnificent. The child begins to laugh hysterically, and on the other side of the closet door, a canister fills up with laugh power.

Where do you get your power?

Elapsed time: Measured from the Pixar logo, this scene begins at 01:20:38 and ends at 01:22:35.

Content: Rated G

Citation: *Monsters, Inc.* (Walt Disney Pictures/Pixar Animation, 2001), written by Dan Gerson and Andrew Stanton, directed by Peter Docter and David Silverman

submitted by David Slagle, Wilmore, Kentucky

57. NEW CREATION

A Knight's Tale

Topic: *Redeemed by the King's Son*

Texts: *Matthew 10:32; 2 Corinthians 5:16–21; Ephesians 2:19; Philippians 3:20–21; 1 Peter 2:9–10*

Keywords: *Heir; Inheritance; Jesus Christ; King; New Creation; Redeemer; Redemption*

In *A Knight's Tale,* William Thatcher (played by Heath Ledger) is a young squire who has always dreamed of being a champion knight and winning jousting tournaments. Unfortunately, as a peasant's son, it's impossible for him to become a noble. However, when his master dies an untimely death, William passes himself off as Sir Ulrich von Lichtenstein and sets out on his quest to become champion of his sport.

In one tournament William Thatcher/Sir Ulrich spares his wounded opponent. He advances to the next round without inflicting further injury. His nemesis, Count Adhemar (played by Rufus Sewell), views William's mercy as weakness and vows to defeat him.

William returns to London, his boyhood home, where he faces Count Adhemar at the world championship. Adhemar discovers William's secret—that he was actually born a thatcher's son in London's Cheapside district. Tipped by Adhemar, the authorities arrest William and display him in public stocks, where the townspeople taunt him.

A man concealed in the crowd emerges from the shadows into the light, removing his cloak. It is the same man whose dignity was spared by William in a former tournament, the knight known as Colville (played by James Purefoy). William and the rest of the crowd are shocked as Colville reveals his true identity. He is actually the Black Prince of Wales—the king's own son.

He says to William, "What a pair we make, both trying to hide who we are, both unable to do so."

The prince orders that William be released and addresses the crowd: "He may appear to be of humble origins, but my personal historians have discovered that he is descended from an ancient royal line. This is my word, and as such is beyond contestation."

He then speaks tenderly to William: "Now, if I may repay the kindness you once showed me. Take a knee." He removes his sword and says, "By the power vested in me by my father, King Edward, and by all the witnesses here, I dub thee, Sir William."

Elapsed time: Measured from the beginning of the opening credit, this scene begins at 01:51:30 and ends at 01:54:24.

Content: Rated PG-13 for brief nudity, sexual connotations, and violence

Citation: *A Knight's Tale* (Columbia Pictures, 2001), written and directed by Brian Helgeland

submitted by Clark Cothern, Tecumseh, Michigan

58. NEW LIFE

The Lord of the Rings: The Two Towers

Topic: *Winning the Struggle against Our Sin Nature*

Texts: *Romans 6:5–7; Romans 8:1; Ephesians 4:22; Colossians 3:9*

Keywords: *Compassion; Freedom; New Heart; New Life; New Man; Self-Condemnation; Sinful Nature; Struggle against Sin*

In *The Lord of the Rings: The Two Towers,* Gollum, also known as Sméagol, is the most pitiful and wretched creature in all of Middle Earth. Frodo, the story's hero (played by Elijah Wood), meets Gollum (played by Andy Serkis) and offers him something he hasn't experienced in years, namely, compassion. In response, Gollum refers to Frodo as his master.

As Gollum experiences Frodo's genuine kindness, Gollum's old, unfriendly nature surfaces. Gollum's old self and new self battle. His old nature is condemning and depraved; his new nature is kind and gentle. Sitting alone on a rock in the dark, a conversation between the two begins.

Old Gollum questions the hobbits' kindness. He says, "Sneaky little hobbitses, wicked, tricksy, filthsss."

But the new Gollum interjects, "No! No! Master!"

"Yes!" the old Gollum hisses. "They will cheat you, hurt you, lie!"

"Master's my friend," new Gollum says plaintively.

Gollum's old self says, "You don't have any friends. Nobody likes you!"

Covering his ears in defiance, new Gollum says, "Not listening! Not listening!"

Old Gollum says, "You're a liar, and a thief!"

"Nope!" the newer, nicer Gollum says.

"Murderer!" the vindictive Gollum says.

"Go away," he begs.

As this exchange continues, the new Gollum shouts out, "We don't need you!"

"What?" asks the old Gollum in disbelief.

Stronger now, the new Gollum asserts himself. "Leave now and never come back!"

To his amazement, the old Gollum is gone. He is unshackled from the wickedness of his old ways.

Relief floods his countenance as he dances and leaps. "We told him to go away! And away he goes. Gone, gone, gone, Sméagol is free!"

Elapsed time: Measured from the beginning of the opening credit, this scene begins at 1:14:44 and ends at 1:16:16.

Content: Rated PG-13 for epic battle sequences and mature themes

Citation: *The Lord of the Rings: The Two Towers* (New Line Cinema, 2002), written by Fran Walsh, Philippa Boyens, Stephen Sinclair, and Peter Jackson (based on the novel by J. R. R. Tolkien), directed by Peter Jackson

submitted by David Slagle, Wilmore, Kentucky

59. NEW LIFE

Regarding Henry

Topic: *Starting a New Life*

Texts: *John 3:3; Romans 12:1–2; 1 Corinthians 6:11; 2 Corinthians 5:17; Colossians 3:12–14*

Keywords: *Conversion; Family; New Heart; New Life; New Man; Repentance*

Regarding Henry tells the story of Henry Morris, a successful lawyer in New York City who has the world by the tail and little time for his family. Whatever it takes to win major court cases, Henry (played by Harrison Ford) will sell his soul for it. Ethical behavior matters less to him than climbing the corporate ladder and maintaining his elaborate lifestyle.

Henry's life changes drastically, though, when he stops at a convenience store late at night and becomes the victim of a robbery. The burglar shoots him in the chest and head. Doctors save his life, but Henry requires months of hospitalization and therapy. He has no memory of his wife, daughter, and colleagues. He enters into an intensive program to reclaim his identity, including wearing clothes he now finds too formal and eating eggs and steak he no longer has a taste for. The process of learning how to walk again is difficult, and so is recapturing his love for his family, who are strangers to him. Eventually he reclaims both.

After resuming his life, Henry discovers some troubling things. He finds evidence that his wife had been unfaithful prior to the shooting.

He is devastated by the news. But he finds out that he had been unfaithful to her as well. What is more, he discovers he withheld evidence in court that prevented a critically ill patient from obtaining a settlement from a hospital Henry was defending.

As the scene begins, Henry returns home, troubled by his past. His wife (played by Annette Bening) meets him at the door and breaks into tears.

"I'm sorry," she says.

"No, I'm sorry," he counters, and then adds, "You were right. Things were different. I have something I need to tell you."

"What is it?" she asks.

"I don't like my clothes," he says, sounding childlike but sincere. "Maybe they used to be my favorite, but I don't feel comfortable in them anymore."

"We'll get you new clothes," his wife says smiling. She reaches to embrace him.

"I'm not done," Henry says, pulling away from her embrace. "Eggs. I don't like eggs, or steak. And Sarah, I hate being a lawyer. I quit, and I told Charlie good-bye."

"Whatever you want is fine," Sarah assures him.

"I want us to be a family for as long as we can, Sarah," Henry quietly whispers. "For as long as we can."

"I love you," she offers.

"I love you, too," Henry says as they embrace.

Elapsed time: Measured from the beginning of the opening credit, this scene begins at 01:40:38 and lasts approximately two minutes.

Content: Rated PG-13 for profanity and sexual content

Citation: *Regarding Henry* (Paramount Pictures, 1991), written by Jeffrey Abrams, directed by Mike Nichols

submitted by Greg Asimakoupoulos, Naperville, Illinois

60. OBEDIENCE

Pearl Harbor

Topic: *Trusting the Father's Orders*

Texts: *Genesis 12:1–10; Genesis 22:1–19;
Proverbs 3:5–6; Matthew 10:5–42; John
21:20–23; 2 Corinthians 5:7; Hebrews 11*

Keywords: *Calling; Church Leaders; Courage; Direction;
Duty; Dying to Self; Faith; Guidance; Leadership;
Ministry; Obedience; Trust*

Pearl Harbor tells of the events leading up to and immediately following the Japanese attack on the United States on December 7, 1941. The film follows the fictional lives of two fighter pilots, Rafe and Danny, who have been inseparable friends since childhood and are stationed at the same base in Hawaii.

Following the attack on Pearl Harbor, Rafe (played by Ben Affleck) and Danny (played by Josh Hartnett) are called into Colonel Jimmy Doolittle's office. They have succeeded in downing seven Japanese planes.

Doolittle (played by Alec Baldwin) stands behind his desk and addresses the cocky pilots somberly.

"You've both been awarded the Silver Star. You're just about the only pilots with combat experience. I need you for a mission I've been ordered to put together."

Rafe and Danny look nervously pleased. Doolittle looks them over carefully.

"Do you know what 'top secret' is?" he asks.

Rafe responds with a wry smile. "Yes, sir! It's the kind of mission when you get medals but they send them to your relatives."

Ignoring the remark, Doolittle continues, "Top secret means you train for something never done before in aviation history—and you go without knowing where you're going. You do it on that basis, or not at all."

Honored to be asked, yet unsure of what they are committing to, both men agree to go.

In many ways, God recruits us to follow him in the same way that Doolittle recruited these pilots for this mission. God trains us in ways unique to us to fulfill unique purposes, and we know little or nothing about where we are going. We go on that basis, or we don't go at all.

[The mission, called Doolittle's Raid, was to attack Japan by air. It was successful, and it affected the course of the war. In the movie, the two pilots lived through the attack, but both were forced to crash-land their planes in China. At this point, Danny was ambushed and killed by Japanese soldiers who had invaded that part of China. Rafe survived.]

Elapsed time: Measured from the beginning of the opening credit, this scene begins at 02:19:35 and ends at about 02:20:20.

Content: Rated PG-13 for battle scenes, images of the wounded, sensuality, and some language

Citation: *Pearl Harbor* (Touchstone Pictures, 2001), written by Randall Wallace, directed by Michael Bay

submitted by Greg Asimakoupoulos, Naperville, Illinois

61. OUTCASTS

For the Birds

Topic: *Fallout of Clique Mentality*

Texts: *Exodus 22:21; Isaiah 58:6–8; Matthew 25:34–45; Romans 15:7; Ephesians 4:3*

Keywords: *Arrogance; Church; Community; Conflict; Cruelty; Factions; Faultfinding; Outcasts; Peer Pressure; Popularity; Rejection; Relationships*

In the Pixar short *For the Birds,* several little bluebirds are sitting on a power line, yapping, squabbling, and jockeying for space, when a large bird gets their attention. He's sitting on a nearby telephone pole, and he looks a little goofy. He gives a friendly chirp. His greeting is met with derision and laughter. The little birds murmur and mock, while the large bird remains oblivious to their cruelty.

Wanting to join the others, the large bird flies over and sits between all of them on the line. His weight causes the line to dip significantly. His intrusion into their world is now met not only with teasing, but also with aggression. The other birds peck-peck-peck at his feet until he finally drops off the line.

The cliquish little birds realize too late their hostile behavior toward the outsider will cause their doom. The large bird's sudden departure from the line causes an upheaval that sends the little birds up in the air like a slingshot. Feathers fly, leaving all the spiteful little birds to land naked and bickering on the ground.

Elapsed time: This short is included with the film *Monsters, Inc.* (Walt Disney Pictures/Pixar Animation, 2001), and appears just prior to the feature presentation. It lasts approximately three minutes.

Content: Not rated

Citation: *For the Birds* (Pixar Animation, 2000), directed by Ralph Eggleston

submitted by David Slagle, Wilmore, Kentucky

62. OUTREACH

How the Grinch Stole Christmas

Topic: *Befriending the Outcast*

Texts: *Leviticus 19:33–34; Matthew 5:43–47; Matthew 28:18–20; Luke 15:1–10; Luke 19:10; Romans 5:6; Ephesians 4:32; 1 Timothy 1:15; 1 Peter 3:8–14; 1 John 4:19–21*

Keywords: *Acceptance; Christmas; Compassion; Evangelism; Great Commission; Law; Love; Mercy; Outreach; Pharisees; Understanding*

How the Grinch Stole Christmas is based on the classic holiday poem by Dr. Seuss. The Grinch (played by Jim Carrey) is a cantankerous, self-centered beast who looks down on the town of Whoville from his home on top of a mountain of garbage. What he sees disgusts him. The people of Whoville (called Whos) love Christmas and all its trappings so much that their lives revolve around celebrating it. The Grinch, however, detests Christmas and the Whos, because when he was a child, the Whos made fun of his odd looks and criticized his homemade Christmas gift. The Whos likewise hate the Grinch.

Cindy Lou (played by Taylor Momsen) is a sweet little Who who interviews people in town to discover how the Grinch came to be so unkind. Based on her research, she feels that the Grinch has been misunderstood. She determines to cross the border of hatred and extend love and acceptance to the beast.

As the townspeople gather for the annual Whobulation, excitement fills the air. Mr. Maywho, the mayor (played by Jeffrey Tambor), steps to the podium to invite nominations for the Holiday Cheermeister. This is a coveted award given to the citizen of the town who seems most deserving. It customarily goes to the egomaniacal mayor.

The mayor declares, "And now the nominations for the Whoville Holiday Cheermeister. Who among us best characterizes the qualities for Whodom? Do I hear a nomination?"

Cindy Lou surprises everyone when, far back in the huddled crowd, she raises her sweet voice. "I nominate the Grinch!" she says.

The townspeople scoff. The mayor mocks. "My, what an altruistic daughter you have there, Lou!" he says sarcastically to Cindy Lou's father.

In pompous style the mayor continues, "Cindy, let me quote a verse from the Book of Who: 'The term *Grinch* will apply when Christmas spirit is in short supply.' Now, I ask you, does that seem like the Holiday Cheermeister?"

"True, Mr. Maywho," Cindy responds. "But the Book of Who says this too: 'No matter how different a Who may appear, he will always be welcomed with holiday cheer.'"

The people look on to see what the mayor will say. He makes up excuses, pretending to quote from the Book of Who.

Little Cindy refuses to be denied. She approaches the mayor and says, "The Book does say, 'The Cheermeister is the one who deserves a backslap or a toast, and goes to the soul at Christmas who needs it the most.' And I believe that soul is the Grinch."

Turning to the silenced crowd, she adds, "And if you're the Whos I think you are, I think you'll think so, too."

The gathered throng supports Cindy Lou's nomination, while Mayor Maywho wrings his hands and shakes his head in disbelief.

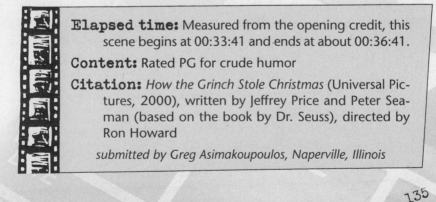

Elapsed time: Measured from the opening credit, this scene begins at 00:33:41 and ends at about 00:36:41.

Content: Rated PG for crude humor

Citation: *How the Grinch Stole Christmas* (Universal Pictures, 2000), written by Jeffrey Price and Peter Seaman (based on the book by Dr. Seuss), directed by Ron Howard

submitted by Greg Asimakoupoulos, Naperville, Illinois

63. OVERCOMING

Stand and Deliver

Topic: *Leading through Hardship*

Texts: *1 Thessalonians 2:11–12; Hebrews 10:25*

Keywords: *Adversity; Affirmation; Attitude; Challenge; Education; Encouragement; Exhortation; Hardship; Leadership; Mentoring; Motivation; Overcoming; Youth*

Stand and Deliver is based on the true story of Jaime Escalante, a math teacher who, through creative teaching techniques, discipline, compassion, and humor, awakens the potential of a group of inner-city Latinos. In 1982, Escalante (played by Edward James Olmos) leaves a good-paying job as a computer engineer to become a math teacher at Garfield High School in East Los Angeles. During his first year, eighteen students willingly give up their Saturdays and vacations to prepare for the Advanced Placement calculus exam. When they finally take the test, Escalante's students unexpectedly pass with flying colors. These unprecedented high marks from this particular Hispanic demographic prompt suspicious testing officials to disqualify the scores, alleging that the students cheated. The only way the students can prove they didn't cheat is to retake the test. They reluctantly agree to take it again.

Crowded in a classroom in the sweltering summer heat, the kids huddle around their teacher. Mr. Escalante breaks the news to them that they only have one day to prepare.

"We're going to have to review the entire course in one shot," he says.

"In one day?" a student asks in disbelief.

Another student chimes in, "Maybe they'll give us the same test."

"No way!" the teacher responds. "It will be harder."

Mr. Escalante begins to pace the classroom and offer encouragement. "Just go step by step and play defense," he advises like a coach in a locker room at halftime. "Don't bring anything. No pencils. No erasers. Nothing. Don't wear clothes with too many pockets. Don't let your eyes wander. No spacing out. Don't give them opportunity to call you cheaters."

He pauses, takes a breath, and then speaks proudly. "You are the true dreamers, and dreams accomplish wonderful things. You're the best!" Escalante cheers. "Tomorrow you'll prove that you're the champs. Now let's start with chapter one."

He pulls a stick of chalk from his shirt pocket and heads for the blackboard.

Elapsed time: Measured from the beginning of the opening credit, this scene begins at 01:26:45 and ends at 01:27:45.

Content: Rated PG for mild profanity

Citation: *Stand and Deliver* (Warner Brothers, 1988), written by Ramón Menéndez and Tom Musca, directed by Ramón Menéndez

submitted by Greg Asimakoupoulos, Naperville, Illinois

64. PARENTING

Smoke Signals

Topic: Sin's Impact on Children

Texts: Proverbs 20:1; Proverbs 23:20–21; Proverbs 23:31–35; Ephesians 5:18

Keywords: Abuse; Addiction; Alcoholism; Drinking; Drunkenness; Family; Parenting; Sin

Smoke Signals tells about two friends, Victor (played by Adam Beach) and Thomas (played by Evan Adams), who were both saved as infants from a 4th of July fire in 1976. The fire claimed many lives on the Coeur d'Alene Indian reservation in Idaho, and Thomas is raised by his grandmother because both his parents were killed. Victor is raised by his single mother after his alcoholic father deserts them. When Victor learns that his estranged father has died, the two friends travel together by bus to Arizona.

En route to Arizona, Victor and Thomas share memories of Victor's dad. Victor reminisces about a time when he was twelve years old and found his mom and dad still in their street clothes passed out on top of their bed.

Empty beer bottles line the chest of drawers and nightstand in their filthy bedroom. While his parents sleep off their hangover, Victor heaves unopened bottles of beer against the house. Victor's mother awakens and realizes he is responding to their behavior. She shouts at her sleeping husband, "We ain't doing this no more! No more! We're done with it!"

Later, while his parents bicker, Victor watches an old Western in black and white. His father attempts to snag his wife's purse. He pleads, "Ginger, all I want is the money I have coming to me."

"It's over!" she shouts. "No more drinking. Do you hear me?"

"Let go!" he counters, pulling the purse away and hitting her in the face.

"Hit me again," Victor's mom cries out in pain. "Come on!"

Her husband storms out of the house heading for his pickup. He throws his suitcase in the back of the pickup. In the background, his wife hollers, "If you leave now, don't ever come back. Do you hear me? Don't you ever come back."

As he starts the engine and begins to pull away, Victor runs from the house calling out, "Don't leave, Dad!" He proceeds to jump in the bed of the pickup as it pulls away. His dad slams on the brakes, jumps out of the car, and pulls his son down. He hugs him one last time before getting back in the truck and driving away. Victor and his mom embrace as they watch the pickup disappear in a cloud of dust.

Elapsed time: Measured from the beginning of the opening credit, this scene begins at 00:30:10 and ends at about 00:32:40.

Content: Rated PG-13 for profanity and mature themes

Citation: *Smoke Signals* (Miramax Films, 1998), written by Sherman Alexie (based on his book *The Lone Ranger and Tonto Fistfight in Heaven*), directed by Chris Eyre

submitted by Greg Asimakoupoulos, Naperville, Illinois

65. POWER

The Rookie

Topic: *Unaware of Strength*

Texts: *Matthew 17:20–21; Mark 11:20–24; Luke 17:6; Acts 1:8; Romans 1:16; Ephesians 1:19–22; Ephesians 3:14–21; Ephesians 6:10; 2 Timothy 1:7; 2 Peter 1:3*

Keywords: *Evangelism; Faith; Power; Prayer*

The Rookie is based on the true story of Jimmy Morris, a high school teacher and baseball coach who became a major league baseball pitcher. Several of the high school players who had been on the receiving end of Morris's fastballs encouraged him to try out for the Tampa Bay Devil Rays. Because of his age and past injuries, Morris (played by Dennis Quaid) dismissed their encouragement as wishful thinking. Morris knew the major league scouts wouldn't consider a prospect unless he could throw 90 miles per hour.

Inwardly, however, Morris can't shake his curiosity. While driving his pickup down a deserted country highway, Morris spots a sign that displays the speed of oncoming traffic. Morris slows his truck and pulls to the side of the road. Looking to see if anyone is watching, Morris grabs a baseball, walks into the road, and tosses the ball past the sign. The number 46 quickly flashes on the sign. It works.

Morris smiles and walks swiftly back to the truck to grab an old baseball glove and another baseball. A car drives down the highway, and Morris quickly turns and leans nonchalantly against his truck. He walks back onto the road and takes one more look to see if any cars are coming. Then he winds up and throws the ball with everything he has. The sign stares blankly back at him for a moment, and then it flashes a 76.

Discouragement falls over Morris's face. He walks slowly to retrieve the baseballs. What Morris does not see is the sign blinking for a moment, and the 7 becoming a 9. Morris has actually thrown a fastball at 96 miles per hour! Yet he remains unaware of his own strength.

Elapsed time: Measured from the beginning of the opening credit, this scene begins at 00:34:52 and ends at 00:37:47.

Content: Rated PG for mild profanity

Citation: *The Rookie* (Walt Disney Pictures, 2002), written by Mike Rich (based on the book *The Oldest Rookie* by Jim Morris and Joel Engel), directed by John Lee Hancock

submitted by David Slagle, Wilmore, Kentucky

Anne of Green Gables

Topic: *Learning to Pray*

Texts: *Matthew 6:9–15; Luke 11:1–13;
Romans 8:26–27*

Keywords: *Children; Devotional Life; Knowing God;
Prayer; Reverence; Spiritual Disciplines*

Anne Of Green Gables features Anne Shirley (played by Megan Follows), an orphan child who is beginning to lose hope that she will ever be placed in the family of her dreams.

One day she finally receives news that she is being placed in a home—that of Marilla Cuthbert (played by Colleen Dewhurst) and Matthew Cuthbert (played by Richard Farnsworth), a brother and sister who live in a picturesque place called Green Gables. It appears that Anne's dreams are finally coming true.

But there's one problem. Marilla and Matthew have specifically asked the orphanage for a little boy—not a girl. Marilla is determined to send Anne back. Anne, of course, is devastated. She'll do anything to stay—even pray, which is something she doesn't know anything about.

In one scene, Ms. Cuthbert asks, "Have you said your prayers?"
Anne responds, "I never say any prayers."

"What do you mean? Haven't you been taught to say your prayers?"

Anne replies, "Mrs. Hammond told me that God made my hair red on purpose, and I've never cared for him since."

"Well," says Anne's new guardian, "while you're under my roof you will say your prayers."

"Why, of course," Anne says, "if you want me to. How does one do it?"

"Well, you kneel beside the bed."

Anne interrupts, "That's the part I never really could understand. Why must people kneel down to pray? If I really wanted to pray, I'd go out into a great big field, all alone. I'd look up into the sky. I'd imagine it was the dome of a great cathedral. Oh, and then I'd close my eyes and just feel the prayer. What am I to say?"

"Well," answers Marilla, "I think you're old enough to think of your own prayer. You thank God for his blessings, and then humbly ask him for the things you want."

"I'll do my best. 'Dear gracious heavenly Father, I thank you for everything. As for the things I especially want, they're so numerous it would take a great deal of time to mention them all. So I'll just mention the two most important. Please let me stay at Green Gables. Please make me beautiful when I grow up. I remain yours respectfully, Anne Shirley—with an *e*.' Did I do all right?"

Ms. Cuthbert replies, "Yes, if you were addressing a business letter to the catalog store. Get into bed."

Anne says, "I should have said 'amen' instead of 'yours respectfully.' Think it'll make any difference?"

"I expect God will overlook it—this time. Good night."

"Good night, Ms. Cuthbert."

Ms. Cuthbert mumbles, "That girl is next door to a perfect heathen."

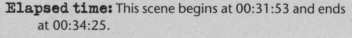

Elapsed time: This scene begins at 00:31:53 and ends at 00:34:25.

Content: Not rated

Citation: *Anne of Green Gables* (Walt Disney Pictures, 1985), written by Kevin Sullivan and Joe Wiesenfeld (based on the novel by Lucy Maud Montgomery), directed by Kevin Sullivan

submitted by Van Morris, Mount Washington, Kentucky

67. PREJUDICE

School Ties

Topic: *Careless Words Reveal Prejudice*

Texts: *Psalm 19:14; John 13:34–35; Romans 15:7; Galatians 3:28; Colossians 3:11; James 2:1–9; James 3:2–9*

Keywords: *Acceptance; Bigotry; Conflict; Confrontation; Friendship; Jewish People; Prejudice; Racism; Tongue; Words*

School Ties is about 1950s small-town, working-class teen David Greene, who receives a football scholarship to St. Matthews, an exclusive prep school. His friendships become strained when another student reveals that David is Jewish.

In this scene, David (played by Brendan Fraser) enters his dorm room, where Chris Reece is studying. Chris (played by Chris O'Donnell) says he is disappointed that David kept his religion a secret. David defiantly says, "You never told me what religion you are."

"I'm Methodist," says Chris.

"You're Methodist? And all the time I didn't know it," David responds sarcastically.

Chris argues that there's a difference, and David demands to know what it is.

Chris says, "It just is. Jews are different. It's not like the difference between Methodists and Lutherans. I mean, Jews—everything about them is different."

David, now angry, demands, "Okay, let's get it out. You think all Jews are dirt, right?"

Chris shakes his head. "Come on, David."

David grabs the front of Chris's shirt and shouts, "No, you come on! You admit it to my face! Jews are greedy, money—" They struggle for a moment. Then David turns and walks broodingly to the other side of the room.

With his cracking voice, he says, "The first day I came to this place, I thought I was dreaming. I knew it was only going to be for a year but, man, what a year. I get into Harvard. And it's not all that easy when you come from a public high school. You guys were my friends. We were winning games. I met Sally. I didn't want to mess it up. I didn't want to be told I couldn't be a part of it because I was a Jew. Can you understand that? It's happened before."

Chris calmly says, "You could have told us. It wouldn't have made a difference."

"Sure, Reece. I knew that first night I got here, when I heard how McGivern got his hi-fi. He 'jewed' him down, remember? Sure it wouldn't make a difference."

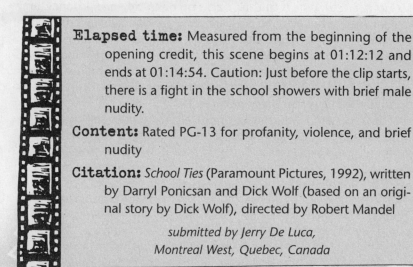

Elapsed time: Measured from the beginning of the opening credit, this scene begins at 01:12:12 and ends at 01:14:54. Caution: Just before the clip starts, there is a fight in the school showers with brief male nudity.

Content: Rated PG-13 for profanity, violence, and brief nudity

Citation: *School Ties* (Paramount Pictures, 1992), written by Darryl Ponicsan and Dick Wolf (based on an original story by Dick Wolf), directed by Robert Mandel

submitted by Jerry De Luca,
Montreal West, Quebec, Canada

68. PREJUDICE

Stand and Deliver

Topic: *The Harm of Assuming the Worst*

Texts: *1 Corinthians 13:7–8*

Keywords: *Assumptions; Betrayal; Brotherly Love; Discouragement; Education; Expectations; Falsehood; Prejudice; Relationships; Self-Pity; Students; Teachers; Trust*

Stand and Deliver is based on the true story of Jaime Escalante. In 1982, Escalante (played by Edward James Olmos) leaves a high-paying job as a computer engineer to become a teacher at Garfield High School in East Los Angeles. Through creative teaching techniques, discipline, compassion, and humor, Escalante awakens the potential of delinquency-prone Latinos in an inner-city school.

Eighteen students turn their backs on gang violence, truancy, and self-destructive behavior to prepare for an Advanced Placement calculus exam. They give up Saturdays and summer vacations to study. When they take the test, Escalante's students pass with flying colors. However, the unprecedented high marks coming from low-income Hispanics prompt the testing officials to disqualify the scores, alleging that cheating most likely occurred.

The devastated students begin reverting to their self-destructive patterns, and Mr. Escalante's confidence is shaken. To make matters worse, his car disappears from the school parking lot. Ironically, just like the Educational Testing Service investigators who assume "foul play" among his students, he assumes his car has been stolen.

As the scene opens, he is walking several miles to his home. As he enters the front door, his wife (played by Rosanna DeSoto) calls out to him. He ignores her and goes directly to their bedroom. When his wife finds him, he is sitting on the bed with his head in his hands. His wife sits beside him and says, "Jaime, want to talk about it?"

"I may have made a mistake trying to teach them calculus," he says, looking at the floor.

"Regardless of whether they passed that test or not, Jaime, they learned," she says.

Jaime answers with obvious sarcasm, "Yeah, they learned if you try real hard, nothing changes."

His wife looks up at the ceiling and then toward him. "Quit! If that's all you have left to teach, quit!"

Jaime replies, "You know what kills me is they've lost their confidence in the system that they're now finally qualified to be a part of." After a brief pause, he continues, "I don't know why I'm losing sleep over this. I don't need it. I could make twice the money in less hours and have people treat me with respect."

His wife counters, "Respect? Jaime, those kids love you."

Just then the sound of a car outside the house is heard. The horn honks several times. Jaime hears one of his students call out for him by his nickname: "Hey, Kimo!"

He walks to the bedroom window and looks out. Unable to believe his eyes, he puts on his glasses. His student says, "Check out your ride, man. We fixed it up for you."

Ashamed of thinking his car had been stolen, he stares in disbelief at his VW Bug. It looks better than it did new. The stolen radio has been replaced, as have the vandalized windows, and the crumpled body has been repainted.

Eventually the teens are retested, and the test is so carefully monitored, there is no way the students can possibly cheat. They pass again with outstanding grades.

Elapsed time: Measured from the beginning of the opening credit, this scene begins at 01:17:54 and ends at about 01:21:24.

Content: Rated PG for mild profanity

Citation: *Stand and Deliver* (Warner Brothers, 1988), written by Ramón Menéndez and Tom Musca, directed by Ramón Menéndez

submitted by Greg Asimakoupoulos, Naperville, Illinois

69. PRIDE

In Love and War

Topic: *Pride Causes Unforgiveness and Anger*

Texts: *Psalm 37:8; Proverbs 14:10; Proverbs 27:4; Ecclesiastes 7:9; Matthew 5:22; Ephesians 4:26–27; Hebrews 12:15*

Keywords: *Anger; Bitterness; Disappointments; Forgiveness; Pain; Pride; Rejection; Relationships; Romantic Love; Self-Pity; Stubbornness; Unforgiving Spirit*

In Love and War is based on the World War I experiences of author Ernest Hemingway. The eighteen-year-old Hemingway (played by Chris O'Donnell) is a Red Cross volunteer in Italy just before the end of the war. While stationed there, he meets, falls in love with, and proposes to Red Cross nurse Agnes von Kurowsky (played by Sandra Bullock). But Agnes, unbeknownst to Hemingway, accepts a marriage proposal from an Italian doctor after Hemingway returns to America. When Hemingway finds out, he is brokenhearted. Agnes later cancels the wedding, realizing she really loves Hemingway.

Agnes travels to Hemingway's lakeside cottage to declare her love for him. As they stand on the veranda, Hemingway, bitter over Agnes's previous rejection of him, turns his back on her. He says nothing. Agnes slides up next to him and declares, "I'll love you as long as I live." But Hemingway does not reciprocate. Instead, he walks into the cottage, bangs his hand on the table in frustration, and covers his eyes in anguish. Agnes sadly walks away.

Agnes narrates the film's conclusion: "I never saw Ernie again after Walloon Lake. I often wonder what might have happened if he had taken me in his arms. But I guess his pride meant he wasn't able to forgive me. Some say he lived with the pain of it all his life. The hurt boy became the angry man—a brilliant, tough adventurer who was the most famous writer of his generation. And the kid who had been, eager, idealistic, and tender, lived on only in my heart."

Ernest Hemingway married four times and took his life in 1961.

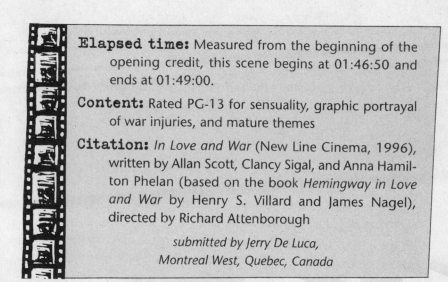

Elapsed time: Measured from the beginning of the opening credit, this scene begins at 01:46:50 and ends at 01:49:00.

Content: Rated PG-13 for sensuality, graphic portrayal of war injuries, and mature themes

Citation: *In Love and War* (New Line Cinema, 1996), written by Allan Scott, Clancy Sigal, and Anna Hamilton Phelan (based on the book *Hemingway in Love and War* by Henry S. Villard and James Nagel), directed by Richard Attenborough

submitted by Jerry De Luca,
Montreal West, Quebec, Canada

70. PRIORITIES

The Man in the Gray Flannel Suit

Topic: *Regret over Living for Work*

Texts: *Exodus 20:3; Deuteronomy 5:7; Psalm 127:2; Proverbs 23:4; Ecclesiastes 5:10–12; Matthew 7:24–29*

Keywords: *Ambition; Balance; Business; Career; Failure; Family; Fatherhood; Goals; Health; Idolatry; Leadership; Marriage; Mistakes; Priorities; Regret; Success; Wisdom; Work*

One of the main characters in *The Man in The Gray Flannel Suit* is Ralph Hopkins (played by Fredric March), president of the United Broadcasting Corporation. Hopkins has been a success by the world's standards. He heads a major corporation, he's wealthy, and he's well-known. He has poured his entire life into his work.

But all is not well with Ralph Hopkins. Ralph's health is not good. His doctor recommends that he sleep more and work less. In nearly every scene we see Ralph in search of a drink. Though Ralph has been a success at business, his personal life has been a dismal failure. Though the word *divorce* is not used, it's clear Ralph and his wife share no intimacy. In fact, though they are cordial, they live in separate homes.

In a particularly sad yet moving scene, Ralph Hopkins reveals his life's "mistake" to one of his employees, Tom Rath (played by Gregory Peck).

"You know where I made my mistake?" Ralph asks. "And yet somebody's got to do it. Somebody's got to dedicate himself to it. Big successful businesses just aren't built by men like you: nine-to-five, home and family. You live on 'em, but you never build one. Big successful businesses are built by men like me. We give everything we've got to it, lift it up regardless of anybody or anything else. And without men like me there wouldn't be any big successful businesses.

"My mistake was in being one of those men."

Elapsed time: This scene begins at 02:02:15 and ends at 02:03:10.

Content: Not rated

Citation: *The Man in the Gray Flannel Suit* (20th Century Fox, 1956), written and directed by Nunnally Johnson (based on the novel by Sloan Wilson)

submitted by Van Morris, Mount Washington, Kentucky

71. PROVIDENCE

Lawrence of Arabia

Topic: *God's Providence and Human Responsibility*

Texts: *Matthew 10:29–31; Matthew 12:11–18; Matthew 28:18–20; John 15:12–13; Romans 9:1–11:36*

Keywords: *Caring; Compassion; Convictions; Courage; Fatalism; God's Sovereignty; Human Worth; Love; Ministry; Providence; Responsibility*

Lawrence of Arabia is based on the true-life adventures of T. E. Lawrence (played by Peter O'Toole), a British military officer who had a passion for the people and land of the Middle East. During World War I he courageously united several enemy Arab tribes into a powerful guerrilla army that defeated the ruling Turkish Empire.

In one scene Lawrence, Sherif Ali ibn el Kharish (played by Omar Sharif), and a group of Arabs ride their camels on a long and seemingly impossible journey through the scorching desert. They are attempting to reach and defeat Aqaba, a major Turkish stronghold on the other side of the desert.

Lawrence is alerted to a riderless camel walking alongside them. Sherif Ali ibn el Kharish tells him the owner of the camel is someone named Gasim. Lawrence wants to know what happened to him. Sherif Ali answers, "God knows."

Lawrence asks, "Why don't you stop?"

"For what? He will be dead by midday."

Lawrence looks at the riderless camel for a moment, then proclaims, "We must go back."

Sherif Ali objects. "What for? To die with Gasim? In God's name, understand. We cannot go back!"

Lawrence replies. "I can." He taps his camel with a rod and turns it around.

One man tells him, "Gasim's time has come. It is written."

Lawrence vehemently disagrees, "Nothing is written!"

Sherif Ali is angry, calls him an "English blasphemer," and tells him he will never make it to Aqaba.

Lawrence replies defiantly, "I shall be at Aqaba. That is written"— and he points to his head—"in here."

Later in the film, after many brutal hours in the scorching sun, Lawrence finds Gasim and brings him back.

Elapsed time: This scene begins at 01:06:40 and ends at 01:08:32.

Content: PG for violence and mature themes

Citation: *Lawrence of Arabia* (Columbia Pictures, 1962), written by Robert Bolt (based on *The Seven Pillars of Wisdom* by T. E. Lawrence), directed by David Lean

submitted by Jerry De Luca,
Montreal West, Quebec, Canada

72. PROVISION

James and the Giant Peach

Topic: *God Meets Our Greatest Need*

Texts: *Psalm 34:9–10; Psalm 65:4; Psalm 81:10; Psalm 144:12–15; Matthew 6:25–34; 2 Corinthians 9:6–11; Ephesians 3:20; Philippians 4:19; James 1:17*

Keywords: *Abundant Life; Daily Bread; Dependence on God; Experiencing God; Fulfillment; Fullness; God's Faithfulness; God's Goodness; Needs; Provision; Self-Reliance; Spiritual Hunger*

James and the Giant Peach is a fairy tale about an orphan boy, James, who is forced to live with his two cruel aunts. He dreams about escaping to a wonderful place across the ocean his parents had told him about—New York City. When a sympathetic stranger appears with a bagful of magic, James (played by Paul Terry) begins his journey with a giant peach and bizarre, life-size insects.

In one scene, James and his insect friends float on the giant peach as they cross the Atlantic Ocean. A flock of birds holds and propels the peach, each tied to it with string. The centipede says desperately, "Want food. Food." He looks at the grasshopper, who suddenly turns into a block of cheese and a bottle of wine. The centipede rubs his eyes in disbelief and then looks at the worm, who suddenly turns into a mustard-covered hot dog. He shakes his head and looks up at the birds, one of which abruptly turns into a whole cooked chicken. Salivating, he grabs the bird's string and pulls it down. As he attempts to bite into the now live and struggling bird, the ladybug hits him with her purse and insists that he put the bird down. The centipede lets go and complains, "But I'm dying of hunger."

The ladybug responds, "Oh, perhaps I have a bit of soda bread in here." She takes a chunk out of her purse.

Seeing this, the grasshopper says, "Food?" and grabs the bread. He insists, "I need the food. I have a much higher metabolism." He takes a bite as the angry centipede lunges at him. They struggle comically for the chunk before it accidentally bounces off the peach and falls into the ocean.

The worm laments, "We're going to starve. Waste away. And not quickly. Miserably. Painfully."

James, who has silently been watching the feud, presses the peach's surface, which gives way just a bit. He raises his hands and happily announces, "Nobody's going to starve! Don't you see? We have enough food here for five voyages."

He climbs down a small hole in the peach, then quickly reemerges with a big chunk of the peach. "The whole ship is made of food." He gives some to the centipede, grasshopper, and ladybug.

The centipede rejoices. "It's the best thing I've ever tasted. And I've tasted a lot."

Elapsed time: Measured from the beginning of the opening credit, this scene begins at 00:36:48 and ends at 00:38:47.

Content: Rated PG for some frightening images

Citation: *James and the Giant Peach* (Walt Disney Pictures, 1996), written by Karey Kirkpatrick, Jonathan Roberts, and Steve Bloom (based on the book by Roald Dahl), directed by Henry Selick

submitted by Jerry De Luca,
Montreal West, Quebec, Canada

73. REALITY

The Truman Show

Topic: *The Need to Face Reality*

Texts: *Ephesians 2:1–7; Philippians 3:18–21; Colossians 3:1–4*

Keywords: *Deception; Emptiness; Freedom; Fulfillment; Meaning of Life; Reality; Temptation; Truth; World*

In *The Truman Show*, Truman (played by Jim Carrey) isn't aware that since birth he has been the star of the ultimate TV reality show. He doesn't know he lives in a large dome built over several square miles. The producer controls the sun, wind, rain, and even ocean waves with the push of a button. A cast of thousands surrounds Truman, but he has no idea every person in his life is simply an actor.

In his thirties now, Truman has become increasingly restless and suspicious. But for the show to continue, he must remain ignorant of the fact that he lives in an artificial world with artificial relationships.

Near the end of the movie, Truman begins to understand his situation and tries to escape. He boards a sailboat and begins to sail away. The cameras follow him, and the producer creates tidal wives to keep Truman from reaching the outer perimeter of his artificial world.

Yet it finally happens—Truman's sailboat touches the horizon that is nothing more than a painted canvas. His suspicions confirmed, he steps off the boat into knee-deep water. Grief etches his face as the truth of his artificial life is revealed. He sees a staircase and ascends to the top, where he finds an exit door.

For the first time ever, the producer (played by Ed Harris) comes over the loudspeaker and begins to speak to Truman. "Truman?" the producer says.

"Who are you?" Truman asks in return.

"I am the creator of the television show that gives hope and joy and inspiration to millions."

"Then who am I?" Truman asks.

"You are the star."

"Was nothing real?"

"You were real," the producer responds.

At this point Truman starts to walk toward the exit door. The frantic producer, who has enslaved Truman for years, begins to unleash a torrent of lies to diminish Truman's courage. He knows that if he can create enough doubt in Truman's mind, Truman will forfeit freedom. "There's no more truth out there than there is in the world I created for you," he says. "The same lies. The same deceit. But in my world you have nothing to fear. You're afraid—that's why you can't leave."

Truman stands at the doorway to real life. While the dome world is artificial, it is all he has ever known. A real, abundant life awaits, but a competing voice with selfish motives urges him to stay in the artificial world.

Elapsed time: This scene begins at 01:29:02 and ends at 01:33:12. Caution: At the end of this scene (at 01:34:00), a character utters a profanity.

Content: Rated PG for brief profanity

Citation: *The Truman Show* (Paramount Pictures, 1998), written by Andrew Niccol, directed by Peter Weir

submitted by David Slagle, Wilmore, Kentucky

74. RECONCILIATION

The Color Purple

Topic: *A Prodigal Returns*

Texts: *Luke 15:11–32; John 8:2–11; 2 Corinthians 5:16–21; Colossians 3:12–14*

Keywords: *Conversion; Family; Forgiveness; Hardness of Heart; Hearing God; Home; Reconciliation; Repentance*

The Color Purple, based on Alice Walker's Pulitzer Prize-winning novel, depicts the rural South in the early 1900s.

Shug Avery (played by Margaret Avery) has lived a rebellious life and broke her pastor-father's heart to follow her dream of becoming a nightclub singer. Pastor Avery, fearing that acknowledging her would be viewed as endorsing her lifestyle, has refused to speak to her for years.

On a summer Sunday evening, Shug is singing at the local juke joint, which is only a few hundred yards from the country church where her father is preaching. His sermon is on how everyone has been a prodigal at some time. The choir begins to sing "God Is Trying to Tell You Something," and their voices can be heard at Shug's open-air club. Shug begins to sing the lyrics of the song she's known since childhood.

She begins walking from the club toward the church. The club patrons follow her in single file. As Shug flings open the door of the church and walks down the center aisle, she continues to sing, "God is trying to tell you something."

Her father stares at his grown daughter, and his face softens. The words of the gospel song penetrate his heart. After years of ignoring his hurting daughter, he realizes God is indeed trying to get his attention. He removes his glasses and steps down from the platform.

Shug races to her dad and embraces him. He wraps his arms around her in forgiveness, and Shug begins to weep.

Elapsed time: This scene begins at 02:22:30 and ends at about 02:26:30.

Content: Rated PG-13 for violence and adult situations

Citation: *The Color Purple* (Warner Brothers, 1985), written by Menno Meyjes (based on the novel by Alice Walker), directed by Steven Spielberg

submitted by Greg Asimakoupoulos, Naperville, Illinois

75. REJECTION

Marty

Topic: *Dealing with Rejection*

Texts: *1 Samuel 16:7; Isaiah 45:9–12; John 7:24; Ephesians 2:10*

Keywords: *Appearance; Dating; Despair; Destiny; Disappointments; Family; Hope; Hopelessness; Human Body; Loneliness; Marriage; Men; Mothers; Rejection; Relationships; Romance; Self-Image; Self-Pity; Self-Worth*

Marty, the 1955 Oscar winner for Best Picture, is about a heavy-set, unattractive, thirty-four-year-old single butcher (played by Ernest Borgnine) who is frustrated at not being able to attract a wife.

In one scene, Marty is sitting at the dinner table, and his mother (played by Esther Minciotti) brings him a plate of spaghetti. She sits beside him and asks him about his plans for the evening. He says he's planning to stay home.

His mother suggests (in a thick Italian accent), "Why don't you go to the Stardust Ballroom? It's loaded with tomatoes." Marty laughs at her use of the word *tomatoes* and says it's just a big dance hall and he's been there many times.

She insists, but Marty replies, "Ma, when are you going to give up? You've got a bachelor on your hands. One fact I've got to face is that whatever it is that women like, I ain't got it. I've chased after enough girls in my life. I went to enough dances. I got hurt enough. I don't want to get hurt no more."

He tells her he had just phoned a girl that afternoon but got "brushed off." He had thought he was past the point of getting hurt, but this hurt. With increasing agitation in his voice, he says, "No, Ma, I don't want to go to the Stardust Ballroom, because girls there just make me feel like I was a bug. I have feelings, you know. I've had enough pain. No thanks, Ma." He puts a forkful of spaghetti in his mouth.

With a look of concern on her face, his mother says, "You're going to die without a son."

Marty, now a little more agitated, says, "I'm just a fat little man! Just a fat ugly man!"

His mother, visibly upset at this, says, "You're not ugly!"

Marty is now really upset, shaking his arms up and down as he gets up from the table and says in a loud, angry voice, "I'm ugly! I'm ugly! I'm ugly! Ma, leave me alone!"

He takes a step away from the table, then steps back to his mother and says in a soft, pleading voice, "Ma, what do you want from me? I'm miserable enough as it is." He tells her he will go to the Stardust Ballroom, but in a resigned tone he says, "Do you know what I'm going to get for my trouble? Heartache. A big night of heartache."

He sits down, puts his hand on his mother's hand for a moment, puts another forkful of spaghetti in his mouth, and says with a slight smirk, "Loaded with tomatoes. That's rich."

Elapsed time: This scene begins at 00:16:15 and ends at 00:19:20.

Content: Not rated

Citation: *Marty* (United Artists, 1955), written by Paddy Chayefsky (based on his television play), directed by Delbert Mann

submitted by Jerry De Luca,
Montreal West, Quebec, Canada

76. RESISTING TEMPTATION

A Beautiful Mind

Topic: *Choosing Not to Indulge Certain Thoughts*

Texts: *Matthew 5:29; Romans 6:11–14; Romans 8:5–7; Romans 12:2; 1 Corinthians 10:13; 2 Corinthians 10:5; Ephesians 2:3; Philippians 4:6–8; James 1:13–15; 1 Peter 4:1–6*

Keywords: *Avoiding Sin; Mind; Resisting Temptation; Self-Control; Sin; Sinful Nature; Temptation; Thoughts*

A Beautiful Mind traces the life of John Forbes Nash Jr. (played by Russell Crowe), who is tortured by paranoid schizophrenia. Nash was a genius mathematician studying at Princeton, seeking to discover a truly original idea. He explained his concept of equilibrium in his 1950 dissertation "Non-cooperative Games," which eventually earned him the 1994 Nobel Prize for economics. Long before this, while a student at Princeton, Nash began to experience paranoid schizophrenia. Several delusional characters left him unable to discern reality from hallucination.

His paranoia climaxed while Nash worked as a professor in the early 1950s at M.I.T.'s Wheeler Defense Labs. Nash was recruited to decipher Soviet codes for the United States government, but following his initial experiences with code breaking, he descended into a delusional world where he continued to work for government agent William Parcher (played by Ed Harris).

During this time, Nash's wife, Alicia (played by Jennifer Connelly), admits him to an institution that diagnoses and treats his disease. After shock therapy and medications leave him unable to think through math problems, care for his young son, or be intimate with his wife, Nash determines to get off the medications and reason his way through his severe mental illness. His determination to overcome his illness leads him to reestablish his relationship with Princeton and eventually to resume teaching.

In this scene, Thomas King (played by Austin Pendleton) from the Nobel Committee met with Nash in 1994 to assess his mental state and determine if he would be a suitable Nobel laureate. In their conversation, Nash says to King tongue in cheek, "I am crazy." Then more soberly, "I take the newer medications, but I still see things that are not here. I just choose not to acknowledge them. Like a diet of the mind, I just choose not to indulge certain appetites."

Elapsed time: This scene begins at 02:08:00 and ends at approximately 02:08:30.

Content: Rated PG-13 for profanity and adult content

Citation: *A Beautiful Mind* (DreamWorks, 2001), written by Akiva Goldsman, directed by Ron Howard

submitted by Todd Dugard, Barrie, Ontario, Canada

77. RESTITUTION

Life as a House

Topic: *Making a Wrong Right*

Texts: *Exodus 22:1–15; Numbers 5:7–8;
Isaiah 61:1–3; Joel 2:25; Micah 6:8;
Luke 4:18–19; Luke 18:1–8*

Keywords: *Caring; Compassion; Conscience; Giving;
Guilt; Injustice; Justice; Parenting; Redemption;
Relationships; Restitution*

In *Life as a House,* George, a forty-something employee at an archi-tectural firm, loses his job and his health. When he learns he has only four months to live, the disrepair of his sorrowful life comes into painful focus.

George (played by Kevin Kline) determines to spend the remain-ing weeks of his life building the house he'd always dreamed of. With the help of his estranged teenage son (played by Hayden Chris-tensen) and ex-wife (played by Kristin Scott Thomas), he tears down his shack and builds a beautiful home on the California coast. The restoration of his house is a metaphor of his life.

During this process, George tells his son, Sam, about how his alcoholic father (Sam's grandfather) caused an accident in which a woman was killed and her small child was paralyzed. He aches over the injustice his father caused.

When George dies, he bequeaths the newly built home to Sam. Sam knows in his heart what he needs to do to honor his father's memory and to make restitution to someone who has been denied justice. He locates the paralyzed girl in a rundown trailer park.

As Sam and his mother walk through the trailer park, his mother asks, "Are you sure you want to do this?"

"Yes," says Sam.

"You could keep it and rent it out," his mom suggests.

"This is what he wanted," Sam insists.

His mother says, "I read the letter. You read the will. He wanted you to keep it and live in it someday."

Sam says, "All right, maybe it's not what he wanted. But it's what he was hoping for."

As the scene ends, Sam and his mother encounter the woman in a wheelchair hanging laundry on a clothesline. In a voiceover, George's voice can be heard: "Twenty-nine years ago my father crossed a double line. It changed my life and that of a little girl forever. I just can't stop thinking about it."

Sam says to the woman in the wheelchair, "Excuse me. Would you mind if we sit a moment and talk? My father built you a house."

Elapsed time: Measured from the opening credit, this scene begins at 01:58:00 and ends at 01:59:30.

Content: Rated R for sexuality and language

Citation: *Life as a House* (New Line Cinema, 2001), written by Mark Andrus, directed by Irwin Winkler

submitted by Greg Asimakoupoulos, Naperville, Illinois

78. RESURRECTION OF BELIEVERS

Pinocchio

Topic: *Longing to Be Changed*

Texts: *John 11:25; Romans 8:14–25; 1 Corinthians 15:42–55; 2 Corinthians 5:1–8; 1 Thessalonians 4:13*

Keywords: *Death; Fulfillment; Human Body; Resurrection of Believers; Sanctification; Self-Sacrifice; Spiritual Adoption*

Pinocchio is based on a nineteenth-century children's story about a lonely old woodcarver named Geppetto who carves a little puppet boy and names it Pinocchio. Whenever he sees the marionette, he thinks how wonderful it would be to have a real son.

Upon seeing the wishing star in the sky, Geppetto wishes Pinocchio would become real. That night, the Blue Fairy brings Pinocchio to life, removes his strings, and instructs the wooden boy to shun evil and follow good. But although he has life, Pinocchio is not fully alive—his body is still made of wood. He longs to be a "real" boy.

One day Pinocchio discovers that a gigantic whale has swallowed Geppetto and the family pets. Pinocchio dives in the sea in an attempt to save his father. After helping to free Geppetto, Figaro the cat, and Cleo the goldfish from the belly of the whale, Pinocchio drowns and is washed to shore. Geppetto is brokenhearted and kneels over the boy sobbing.

The Blue Fairy speaks above Pinocchio, "Awake, Pinocchio, awake." Pinocchio is supernaturally transformed from a wooden boy into one who is fully alive, complete with flesh and bones. He sits up and rubs his eyes. Seeing Geppetto weeping over his bed, Pinocchio calls out, "Father! What are you crying for?"

Unable to comprehend what has transpired, Geppetto answers, "Because you are dead, Pinocchio."

Released from his former life, Pinocchio replies, "No, I'm not. I'm alive. See? I'm real. I'm a real boy."

At last, Geppetto is able to see the truth. What appeared to be death was just the opposite. Pinocchio is at last complete.

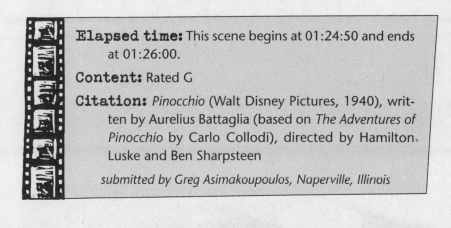

Elapsed time: This scene begins at 01:24:50 and ends at 01:26:00.

Content: Rated G

Citation: *Pinocchio* (Walt Disney Pictures, 1940), written by Aurelius Battaglia (based on *The Adventures of Pinocchio* by Carlo Collodi), directed by Hamilton Luske and Ben Sharpsteen

submitted by Greg Asimakoupoulos, Naperville, Illinois

79. REWARDS

The Inn of the Sixth Happiness

Topic: *The Testimony of Compassion*

Texts: *Psalm 41:1–2; Proverbs 19:17; Isaiah 58:6–14; Matthew 5:13–16; Matthew 10:42; Matthew 20:25–28; Matthew 25:34–40; Titus 2:9–10; 1 Peter 3:1–2*

Keywords: *Compassion; Evangelism; Example; Faithfulness; Love; Ministry; Missions; Outreach; Rewards; Servanthood; Spiritual Strength; Testimony; Witness*

The Inn of the Sixth Happiness is based on the true story of Gladys Aylward (played by Ingrid Bergman), a faithful missionary in a remote Chinese village who helped run an inn for traveling mule drivers. The China Inland Mission Center in England refused to sponsor her because of her lack of vocation and experience, so in 1932 she set out on her own, believing with all her heart that she was called by God.

After Gladys served for many years, the Chinese mandarin (governor) of the town of Yang Cheng (played by Robert Donat) made her the official "foot inspector," a position that required her to convince the town's aristocracy to cease the injurious tradition of binding young women's feet to prevent them from growing. Because of her demonstrated love, she was given the name Jennai, meaning "one who loves people."

When the Japanese army invades northern China, the village mandarin, elders, and Jennai enter a conference room and take a seat around a large circular table. The mandarin offers a toast, saying farewell to the past: "In a little while we must leave our city, perhaps for years, perhaps forever. For those of us who are old, certainly forever. Elders of Yang Cheng, I thank you for your help in this time of trouble. But we were born to our trouble. There is one who has taken it upon herself, not from necessity, but from love."

He stands up, and all the elders follow. Jennai, however, remains seated. "Jennai, we thank you from those who are not here, whose children you have taken as your own, for the poor and the sick and the afflicted, from all the people of Yang Cheng, for the past and for the future. I honor you for your strength. I wish to share with you the faith from which it comes."

Jennai, realizing he is talking about her Christian faith, is overcome with emotion.

"City recorder, close the book of Yang Cheng with this entry: 'As a sign of respect for the honored foot inspector of this city, the Shian Sang of Yang Cheng has become a Christian.'"

Jennai lifts her head slightly and begins to weep openly. "Oh, I thank you for this great gift."

"Jennai," the mandarin says as he puts his hand on her shoulder, "accept my gift. It is offered with love."

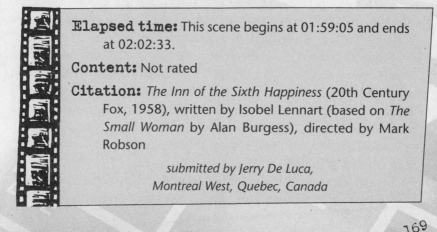

Elapsed time: This scene begins at 01:59:05 and ends at 02:02:33.

Content: Not rated

Citation: *The Inn of the Sixth Happiness* (20th Century Fox, 1958), written by Isobel Lennart (based on *The Small Woman* by Alan Burgess), directed by Mark Robson

submitted by Jerry De Luca,
Montreal West, Quebec, Canada

80. SACRIFICE

Men in Black

Topic: *Worth the Sacrifice*

Texts: *Matthew 16:24–27; Matthew 19:27–30; Mark 1:17–20; Mark 10:29–31; Luke 14:25–33; Luke 18:28–30*

Keywords: *Disciple; Discipleship; Great Commission; Leadership; Ministry; Mission; Missionary; Sacrifice; Service*

*M*en in Black is a comedy about two special agents who work for Men in Black, an underground agency created to protect planet Earth from tyrant extraterrestrials. Agent K (played by Tommy Lee Jones) and Agent J (played by Will Smith), a hotshot New York City cop, partner to exterminate a villainous alien—"the bug."

Before Agent J relinquishes his police badge to join Men in Black, Agent K explains the scenario for Agent J, who is still unsure of what the agency does and what it wants of him.

Agent K explains, "All right, kid, here's the deal. At any given time there are around fifteen hundred aliens on the planet. Most of them are right here in Manhattan. Most are decent enough. They're just trying to make a living. Humans, for the most part, don't have a clue."

Agent J asks, "But, uh, why the big secret? Humans are smart. They can handle it."

Agent K answers: "A person is smart. People are dumb, panicky, dangerous animals, and you know it. Fifteen hundred years ago, everyone knew the earth was the center of the universe. Five hundred years ago, everyone knew the earth was flat. And fifteen minutes ago you knew that people were alone on this universe." With a sigh, Agent K adds, "Imagine what you'll know tomorrow."

J asks, "What's the catch?"

"The catch?" K says. "The catch is you will sever every human contact. Nobody will ever know you exist anywhere. Ever." K pauses and then adds, "I'll give you till sunrise to think it over."

As K strolls away, J shouts, "Hey, is it worth it?"

"Oh yeah, it's worth it," K answers, "If you're strong enough."

Elapsed time: Measured from the beginning of the opening credit, this scene begins at 00:31:10 and ends at 00:32:50.

Content: Rated PG-13 for mild vulgarity and violence

Citation: *Men in Black* (Columbia Pictures, 1997), written by Ed Solomon (based on the comic book by Lowell Cunningham), directed by Barry Sonnenfeld

submitted by Melissa Parks, Des Plaines, Illinois

81. SECURITY

Mr. Mom

Topic: *Surrendering a Security Blanket*

Texts: *Deuteronomy 6:7; Psalm 68:5;
Proverbs 22:6; Ephesians 6:4; Colossians
3:21; 1 Thessalonians 2:11–12*

Keywords: *Children; Fatherhood; Fathers; Guidance;
Parenting; Security*

In *Mr. Mom,* Jack (played by Michael Keaton) and Caroline Butler (played by Teri Garr) are a traditional couple struggling to make ends meet. When Jack loses his job, they decide he should stay home with the kids while his wife works. Jack has no idea what it takes to run the house and raise the kids—which makes for many laughs as he becomes Mr. Mom.

In one scene, Jack is trying to convince his six-year-old boy, Kenny (played by Taliesan Jaffe), that it's time to part with his security blanket—his "woobie." Jack enters Kenny's room and has a heart-to-heart talk with Kenny, who clings to the blanket.

"Listen, Ace," Jack says, "you and I have to have a man-to-man talk about your woobie. Your woobie is looking bad, Bud. I understand that you little guys start out with your woobies, and you think they're great. And they are—they are terrific. But pretty soon a woobie isn't enough. You're out on the street trying to score an electric blanket or maybe a quilt, and the next thing you know, you're strung out on bedspreads. Ken, that's serious."

After a few moments of vain negotiating, Jack says, "Okay, give it to me for a couple of days. If it doesn't work, you get the woobie back. Please?" As Kenny reluctantly hands his father the woobie, Jack says, "You've got a lot of guts."

Elapsed time: Measured from the beginning of the opening credit, this scene begins at 00:58:43 and ends at 01:00:41.

Content: Rated PG for small amounts of profanity

Citation: *Mr. Mom* (20th Century Fox, 1983), written by John Hughes, directed by Stan Dragoti

submitted by Bill White, Paramount, California

82. SECURITY IN GOD

Gods and Generals

Topic: *Serenity in the Midst of Adversity*

Texts: *Psalm 20:7; Psalm 62:1–2; Psalm 91:14–15; Psalm 139:16; Jeremiah 29:11; 2 Corinthians 5:1*

Keywords: *Adversity; Confidence; Danger; Death; Emotions; Eternal Perspective; Faith; God's Sovereignty; Peace; Readiness; Security in God; Trust; War*

The movie *Gods and Generals* follows the rise and fall of Civil War hero General Thomas (Stonewall) Jackson (played by Stephen Lang).

Jackson is a devout Christian. Upon his call to report for duty and lead the 1st Brigade of Virginia (the Stonewall Brigade), Jackson and his wife read from 2 Corinthians 5 and pray for God's will to be done. Again, in the early morning hours of July 21, 1861, the day of the Battle of Manassas Junction, Jackson asks God that his will be done.

In the early stages of the battle, things do not go well for the Confederates. In an attempt to rally the troops, someone yells to the men to look at Jackson "standing like a stone wall." Suddenly, General Jackson, sitting erect in his saddle with cannon fire exploding all around him, his left hand wounded by a musket ball, begins to rally his men. Stunningly brave, he paces back and forth on his horse across the front line, shouting orders to "charge" as musket balls pierce the air.

At the end of the day, General Jackson and his captain return to the battlefield to survey the loss: 111 Confederates dead, 373 missing. Wearied and saddened, Jackson kneels beside a dead soldier with Captain James Smith (played by Stephen Spacek). Captain Smith asks, "General, how is it you can keep so serene and stay so utterly insensible with a storm of shells and bullets raining about your head?"

Jackson replies, "Captain Smith, my religious belief teaches me to feel as safe in battle as in bed. God has fixed the time for my death—I do not concern myself with that, but to be always ready, whenever it should overtake me. That is the way all men should live. Then all men would be equally brave."

Elapsed time: Measured from the beginning of the opening credit, this scene begins at 0:51:22 and ends at 0:52:38.

Content: Rated PG-13 for sustained battle sequences

Citation: *Gods and Generals* (Warner Brothers, 2003), written and directed by Ronald F. Maxwell (based on the book by Jeff Shaara)

submitted by Van Morris, Mount Washington, Kentucky

83. SELF-CONTROL

Raiders of the Lost Ark

Topic: Controlling What We See

Texts: Genesis 19:17–26; Matthew 6:22–23; Luke 11:34–36; 1 John 2:15–17

Keywords: Desire; Self-Control

In *Raiders of the Lost Ark,* Indiana Jones (played by Harrison Ford) and his love interest, Marion (played by Karen Allen), are near the end of their action-packed journey to recover the much sought after Ark of the Covenant. They have been fighting a group of Nazis and a competing archaeologist for possession of the Ark. They are now tied to a post, back-to-back, with the Nazis surrounding them.

They have found the Ark of the Covenant, and the Nazis begin to open it in hopes of finding treasure. At first they see only a pile of sand, but then smoke slowly starts to leak out. The smoke turns into spirits with women's faces. Jones's nemesis, the other archaeologist, declares, "It's beautiful!" as the spirits fly in and around the group. Suddenly there is a series of electrical explosions.

Jones is trying to figure out what's going on. He realizes there may be grave danger ahead because the Ark, a sacred object, has been opened. He shouts to Marion, "Marion, don't look at it! Shut your eyes, Marion. Don't look at it no matter what happens!"

Suddenly everyone who is looking at the spirit disintegrates. The fire and winds reach near hurricane levels. Marion cries at the top of her lungs, "Indy!!!" Jones shouts, "Don't look, Marion! Keep your eyes shut!"

Ultimately everyone except Indiana Jones and Marion are decimated.

Elapsed time: This scene begins at 01:30:00 and ends at 01:32:40.

Content: Rated PG

Citation: *Raiders of the Lost Ark* (Lucasfilm/Paramount Pictures, 1981), written by Lawrence Kasdan (based on a story by George Lucas and Philip Kaufman), directed by Steven Spielberg

submitted by Elaine Larson, Barrington, Illinois

84. SELF-SACRIFICE

Mulan

Topic: *Child's Sacrifice for Father*

Texts: *Mark 10:45; John 10:11; John 15:13; Romans 8:2–4; 1 Corinthians 13:1–7; Philippians 2:1–4; 1 John 4:7–12*

Keywords: *Children; Christ as Substitute; Courage; Family; Honor; Love; Sacrifice; Self-Denial; Self-Sacrifice*

Mulan is a Disney animation based on an ancient Chinese legend in which a girl becomes a national hero through daring acts of self-sacrifice and courage.

When the Huns invade China, the emperor prepares for war. He issues an edict that requires one man from every family in the country to report for duty.

Since the Fa family has only a daughter, Mulan, her elderly and crippled father (voiced by Soon-Tek Oh) knows he must represent the family and go to war. What he lacks in strength the old man compensates for in pride. He is willing and honored to accommodate the emperor's request.

When the regent hands Mr. Fa his orders, Mulan (voiced by Ming-Na Wen) attempts to explain that her father's infirmities make him incapable of joining the campaign. But the regent rebuffs her while her father watches in shame.

Later, Mulan walks past her father's room and sees him standing in front of the military uniform he donned in years past. She watches as he removes his large sword and rehearses the motions of a sword fight. Too weak even to hold his weapon, he collapses to the floor in pain. Mulan is beset with worry; she knows her father is too weak to survive a battle.

As the family sits at dinner in somber silence, Mulan can take it no longer. She throws her rice bowl on the table and says, "You shouldn't have to go. There are plenty of young men to fight for China."

Her father responds, "It is an honor to protect my country and my family."

"So you'll die for honor?" Mulan asks sarcastically.

"I will die doing what is right. I know my place, and it's time you learned yours."

Mulan leaves the room brokenhearted. After contemplating her options, she vows to pass herself off as a man and fight on her father's behalf. She is willing to lay down her life so that he might live.

While her parents sleep, Mulan enters their room and dresses in her father's uniform. She takes her father's written orders and rides off on a horse.

Elapsed time: Measured from the beginning of the opening credit, this scene begins at 00:16:00 and ends at approximately 00:19:25.

Content: Rated G

Citation: *Mulan* (Walt Disney Pictures, 1998), written by Rita Hsiao and Chris Sanders (based on *Fa Mulan: The Story of a Woman Warrior* by Robert San Souci), directed by Tony Bancroft and Barry Cook

submitted by Greg Asimakoupoulos, Naperville, Illinois

85. SERVANTHOOD

Marvin's Room

Topic: *Privileged to Give Love*

Texts: *Luke 10:25–37; John 13:1–17; John 15:12–17; Acts 20:35; Romans 13:8–10; Galatians 5:13–14; 1 Thessalonians 4:9–10; 1 John 4:7–21*

Keywords: *Compassion; Death; Dying to Self; Fulfillment; Generosity; Giving; Love; Meaning of Life; Purpose; Self-Sacrifice; Servanthood; Sorrow; Unselfishness*

*M*arvin's Room is about two sisters, Lee (played by Meryl Streep) and Bessie (played by Diane Keaton). The sisters have been estranged for seventeen years, and now Bessie discovers she has leukemia. Though generally self-centered, Lee visits her sister to test for a bone marrow match. Despite her illness, Bessie, true to form, continues caring for her ailing aunt and father.

When Bessie learns that Lee isn't a match, she tries to remain calm but accidentally knocks over a bottle of pills on the counter.

(Warning: As she does this she begins to utter a profanity, so if you are showing the video, begin here.)

Staring blankly at the pills, Lee asks Bessie if she wants to lie down, but Bessie refuses. They bend down, facing each other, and start picking up the pills. Bessie steals a quick glance at Lee's teary-eyed face. Lee looks up, and they catch each other's eye. A warm and gracious smile exudes from Bessie's face, silently thanking Lee for her concern.

She reassures Lee, "Oh, Lee. I've been so lucky. So lucky to have Dad and Ruth. I've had such love in my life. I look back, and I've had such, such love."

Lee nods, "They love you very much."

Bessie gently shakes her head. "No, that's not what I mean. No. No. I mean that I love them. I've been so lucky to have been able to love someone so much."

Lee nods, not seeming to understand. "Yeah, you are."

They hear some faint grunts coming from another room. Bessie gets up and walks into the room. Their father is lying in bed and looks toward Bessie. She sighs and then gives a big smile.

Elapsed time: Measured from the beginning of the opening credit, this scene begins at 01:26:18 and ends at 01:28:12. Caution: After Bessie knocks over the bottle of pills, she begins to utter a profanity.

Content: Rated PG-13 for mature themes and profanity

Citation: *Marvin's Room* (Miramax Films, 1996), written by Scott McPherson (based on his play), directed by Jerry Zaks

submitted by Jerry De Luca,
Montreal West, Quebec, Canada

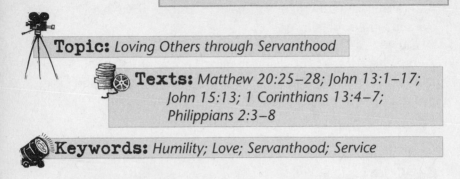

86. SERVANTHOOD

The Princess Bride

Topic: *Loving Others through Servanthood*

Texts: *Matthew 20:25–28; John 13:1–17; John 15:13; 1 Corinthians 13:4–7; Philippians 2:3–8*

Keywords: *Humility; Love; Servanthood; Service*

The *Princess Bride* begins at the home of Buttercup (played by Robin Wright), the future princess bride. Her small, crude house sits on a hill, with beautiful sloping countryside as a backdrop.

Though dressed in drab brown clothes and clearly a peasant girl, Buttercup orders others around as though she were royalty. Another peasant named Westley (played by Cary Elwes) is a laborer on Buttercup's farm, and the narrator says that Buttercup's greatest pleasure in life is tormenting Westley. She refers to him as "farm boy" and makes liberal use of her authority as she orders him about.

Yet no matter how menial the task, Westley always responds the same way: "As you wish."

"Farm boy," Buttercup says, "polish my horse's saddle."

"As you wish."

"Farm boy," she says as she drops two pails at his feet, "fill this with water."

"As you wish."

"Farm boy, fetch me that pitcher."

"As you wish."

Though Buttercup is maddeningly condescending, Westley is the model servant. He never refuses her demands, and his attitude is kind and willing.

The narrator reveals that one day Buttercup has a precious insight. He reads, "That day she was amazed to discover that when he was saying 'As you wish,' what he meant was 'I love you.'"

Elapsed time: This scene begins at 00:02:10 and ends at 00:03:59.

Content: Rated PG for violence and some offensive language

Citation: *The Princess Bride* (20th Century Fox, 1987), written by William Goldman (based on his novel), directed by Rob Reiner

submitted by David Slagle, Wilmore, Kentucky

87. SIGNS AND WONDERS

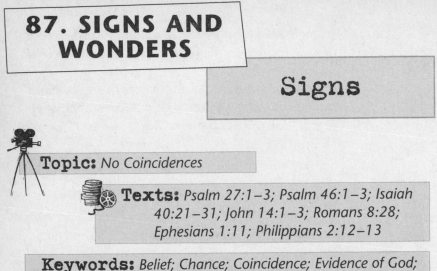

Signs

Topic: No Coincidences

Texts: Psalm 27:1–3; Psalm 46:1–3; Isaiah 40:21–31; John 14:1–3; Romans 8:28; Ephesians 1:11; Philippians 2:12–13

Keywords: Belief; Chance; Coincidence; Evidence of God; Faith; Fear; God's Faithfulness; Hope; Luck; Miracles; Providence; Signs and Wonders

Signs is the story of the Hess family of Bucks County, Pennsylvania, who wake up one morning to find a 500-foot crop circle in the middle of their cornfield. Graham Hess (played by Mel Gibson), his brother Merrill (played by Joaquin Phoenix), and Graham's two children, Morgan and Bo, watch TV news reports with growing alarm as they learn that the crop circle in their cornfield is similar to others around the world—all the products of an alien invasion force. On the TV screen they see fourteen lights in the night sky over Mexico City, visual evidence of the invaders.

Merrill turns to Graham, a former pastor who has lost his faith, for some comfort. "Some people think this is the end of the world," Merrill muses. "Is it true? Do you think it could be?"

"Yes," Graham flatly replies.

Alarmed by his brother's response, Merrill questions, "How can you say that?"

"That wasn't the answer you wanted?" Graham asks.

Full of fear, Merrill demands, "Couldn't you pretend to be like you used to be? Give me some comfort."

Graham explains, "People break down into two groups when they experience something lucky. Group number one sees it as more than luck, more than coincidence. They see it as a sign, evidence that there is someone up there watching out for them. Group number two sees it as just pure luck, a happy turn of chance.

"Sure there are people in group number two looking at those fourteen lights in a very suspicious way. For them, the situation is fifty-fifty. Could be bad, could be good. But deep down, they feel that whatever happens, they're on their own. And that fills them with fear. But there's a whole lot of people in group number one. When they see those fourteen lights, they're looking at a miracle, and deep down they feel that whatever's going to happen, there will be someone there to help them. And that fills them with hope. So what you have to ask yourself is what kind of person are you? Are you the kind that sees signs, sees miracles? Or do you believe that people just get lucky? Or look at the question this way: Is it possible that there are no coincidences?"

Elapsed time: Measured from the opening credits, this scene begins at 00:40:00 and ends at approximately 00:42:00.

Content: Rated PG-13 for language, mature themes, and frightening moments

Citation: *Signs* (Touchstone Pictures, 2002), written and directed by M. Night Shyamalan

submitted by Charles Griffith, Oviedo, Florida

88. SILENCE OF GOD

The Count of Monte Cristo

Topic: *Where Is God in Suffering?*

Texts: *Job 13:15; Psalm 12:5–6; Psalm 13:1–2; Psalm 22:1–5; Habakkuk 1:2–4; Matthew 27:43; 1 Peter 2:19–21*

Keywords: *Circumstances and Faith; Evil; Faith; God's Omnipresence; Injustice; Persecution; Skepticism; Suffering; Trials; Trust; Unbelief*

In *The Count of Monte Cristo*, the hero, Edmond (played by Jim Caviezel), is unjustly imprisoned in the sinister Château d'If (pronounced *deef*). As he enters his cell, escorted by the malevolent warden, Dorleac (played by Michael Wincott), he sees an inscription gouged into the otherwise barren wall: GOD WILL GIVE ME JUSTICE.

"People are always trying to motivate themselves," Dorleac sneers. "Or they keep calendars. But soon they lose interest, they die, and all I am left with is a rather unsightly wall, I'm afraid. So I have conceived another way to help our prisoners keep track of time. Every year on the anniversary of their imprisonment, we hurt them. Usually just a simple beating, really. Although on their first day here—in your case, today—I like to do something rather special."

Dorleac keeps speaking as his assistants chain Edmond and hoist him off the floor by the wrists.

"And if you are thinking just now," Dorleac continues as he prepares his whip, "'Why me, O God?' the answer is, God has nothing to do with it. In fact, God is never seen in France this time of year."

Though obviously terrified, Edmond answers, "God has everything to do with it. He is everywhere; he sees everything."

Dorleac's response is chilling. "All right, let's make a bargain, shall we? You ask God for help, and I'll stop the moment he shows up." And with that he begins to whip the defenseless and innocent Edmond.

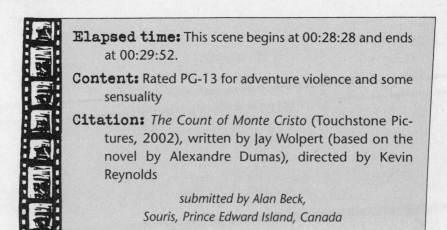

Elapsed time: This scene begins at 00:28:28 and ends at 00:29:52.

Content: Rated PG-13 for adventure violence and some sensuality

Citation: *The Count of Monte Cristo* (Touchstone Pictures, 2002), written by Jay Wolpert (based on the novel by Alexandre Dumas), directed by Kevin Reynolds

submitted by Alan Beck,
Souris, Prince Edward Island, Canada

89. SINFUL NATURE

The Lord of the Rings: The Fellowship of the Ring

Topic: *Overcoming Adam in Us*

Texts: *Romans 5:14–21; Romans 6:6–7; Romans 8:1–14; 1 Corinthians 15:22; 2 Corinthians 5:17–20; Ephesians 4:22–24; Colossians 3:10*

Keywords: *Adam and Eve; Depravity; Fall of Humanity; Human Condition; Humanity; New Man; Overcoming; Resisting Temptation; Sin; Sinful Nature; Weakness*

In *The Lord of the Rings: The Fellowship of the Ring,* Christian author J. R. R. Tolkien portrays the classic conflict between good and evil, set in a mythical land called Middle Earth. After a great battle in ancient times, the Dark Lord Sauron is temporarily defeated, and his most dreaded weapon, the Ring of Power, is lost for many ages.

By seeming happenstance, a hobbit named Frodo Baggins (played by Elijah Woods) finds this ring in his possession. With the help of a small band of warriors—called The Fellowship of the Ring—Frodo embarks on an epic quest to destroy the ring.

One of Frodo's comrades is Aragorn, the only direct heir of the infamous Isildur. Thousands of years before, Isildur won a battle against the Dark Lord, but because of pride, he refused to destroy the ring. Instead, he kept the ring for himself, which ultimately led to his own destruction. The Dark Lord again sought to conquer the world.

Aragorn (played by Viggo Mortensen) is faced with the decision to live in the shame of his past or to emerge from the shadows to fight for what is right. Yet he senses the same pride in himself as in his forefather. Fearful of failure, he considers abandoning the mission. His true love, Arwen (played by Liv Tyler), comes to his side and helps him make the hard choice to enter the battle.

Arwen asks, "Why do you fear the past? You are Isildur's heir, not Isildur himself. You are not bound by his fate."

Choked with fear, Aragon explains, "The same blood flows in my veins. The same weakness."

"Your time will come. You will face the same evil," Arwen affirms, "and you will defeat it."

In a similar way, the blood of Adam and his sinful nature flows in our veins, but through Jesus Christ we are a new creation, able to defeat the power of sin.

Elapsed time: Measured from the beginning of the opening credit, this scene begins at 01:23:00 and ends at 01:24.30.

Content: Rated PG-13 for epic battle sequences and scary images

Citation: *The Lord of the Rings: The Fellowship of the Ring* (New Line Cinema, 2001), written by Fran Walsh, Philippa Boyens, and Peter Jackson (based on the novel by J. R. R. Tolkien), directed by Peter Jackson

submitted by Bill White, Paramount, California

90. STRUGGLING AGAINST SIN

The Lord of the Rings: The Fellowship of the Ring

Topic: *Struggling to Overcome Sin*

Texts: *Matthew 19:16–24; Romans 7:21–25; Colossians 3:5–10; Hebrews 12:3; James 1:13–15; James 4:4; 1 John 2:15–17*

Keywords: *Avoiding Sin; Conviction of Sin; Evil; Overcoming; Resisting Temptation; Sinful Nature; Surrender; Temptation; World; Worldliness*

In *The Lord of the Rings: The Fellowship of the Ring,* author J. R. R. Tolkien portrays the classic conflict between good and evil, set in a mythical land called Middle Earth. After a great battle in ancient times, the Dark Lord Sauron is temporarily defeated, and his most dreaded weapon, the Ring of Power, is lost for many ages.

A hobbit named Bilbo Baggins (played by Ian Holm) finds the ring and, unaware of its true identity, passes it on to his nephew, Frodo, as part of an inheritance. Frodo Baggins, the hero (played by Elijah Wood), is full of humility and uncertainty as he embarks on an epic quest to destroy the ring.

In one scene, Bilbo converses with his wise and trusted friend Gandalf (played by Ian McKellen) about departing on a long journey and leaving his inheritance behind for Frodo. The ring is part of that inheritance, and ever so subtly the ring has begun to exert itself on Bilbo, as it does with everyone who comes near it.

As Gandalf encourages Bilbo to leave the ring behind, Bilbo grasps it and bellows, "It's mine! My own! My precious. What business is it of yours what I do with my own affairs?" Bilbo casts a suspicious eye on Gandalf and accuses, "You want it for yourself!"

Firmly, Gandalf responds, "Bilbo Baggins, do not take me for some conjurer of cheap tricks. I am not trying to rob you! I'm trying to help you. All your long years we've been friends. Trust me, as you once did. Let it go."

Gradually Bilbo's defiance fades, and he embraces Gandalf, saying, "You're right, Gandalf. The ring must go to Frodo."

Elapsed time: Measured from the beginning of the opening credit, this scene begins at 00:20:59 and ends at 00:23:48.

Content: Rated PG-13 for epic battle sequences and scary images

Citation: *The Lord of the Rings: The Fellowship of the Ring* (New Line Cinema, 2001), written by Fran Walsh, Philippa Boyens, and Peter Jackson (based on the novel by J. R. R. Tolkien), directed by Peter Jackson

submitted by Bill White, Paramount, California

91. STUMBLING BLOCKS

Eight Men Out

Topic: *Causing Others to Stumble*

Texts: *Genesis 3:1–6; Matthew 18:7–9; Luke 4:1–13; 1 Corinthians 8:9–13*

Keywords: *Business; Character; Compromise; Consequences; Corruption; Greed; Hypocrisy; Influence; Integrity; Money; Revenge; Sin; Sinful Nature; Sports; Stumbling Blocks; Temptation; Tolerating Sin*

Eight Men Out is the historical drama about the Chicago White Sox scandal of 1919. Many Sox players felt cheated and demoralized by owner Charles Comiskey's penny-pinching, tough-handed ways. Gamblers and hustlers influenced several of them to lose the World Series in exchange for a large amount of money. Eventually the scandal was exposed. Though a jury found them not guilty, the baseball commissioner banned them from the major leagues for life.

In this scene, Chick Gandil (played by Michael Rooker), one of the first players who agrees to "throw" the World Series, tries to convince star pitcher Eddie Cicotte (played by David Strathairn) to join in.

Eddie tells Chick, "Forget it. I make six grand a year. A lot of people are out of work." Chick tells Eddie that he's getting older and his arm won't hold up much longer, that owner Comiskey won't help him if he gets hurt. Eddie firmly refuses the offer.

In the next scene, Eddie stands before Comiskey (played by Clifton James), who is seated at his desk. Eddie calmly and confidently tells him, "You said if I won thirty games this year, there would be a $10,000 bonus. I think you owe it to me." Comiskey asks his assistant how many games Eddie had won that year. The answer: twenty-nine.

Eddie argues that Comiskey had the manager rest him for two weeks in August, resulting in Eddie missing five starts. "I would have won at least two of those games. You know that."

Comiskey insists they had to rest his arm for the Series, claiming, "I have to keep the best interests of the club in mind, Eddie."

Eddie responds in a firmer tone, "I think you owe me that bonus."

Comiskey says calmly, "Twenty-nine is not thirty, Eddie. You will get only the money you deserve." Eddie gives a restrained and unhappy sigh and walks out of the office.

Demoralized, Eddie approaches Chick and tells him, "Ten grand. For the first game. Cash."

Chick replies, "What?"

Eddie says, "You heard me." He gets up and walks away. Chick watches him walk away, and a smile comes across his face.

Elapsed time: Measured from the beginning of the opening credit, this scene begins at 00:22:27 and ends at 00:24:56.

Content: Rated PG for profanity

Citation: *Eight Men Out* (Orion Pictures, 1988), written by John Sayles (based on the book by Eliot Asinof), directed by John Sayles

submitted by Jerry De Luca,
Montreal West, Quebec, Canada

92. TEENAGERS

Rebel Without a Cause

Topic: *Attitude toward Parents*

Texts: *Leviticus 19:3; Malachi 4:6; 1 Corinthians 13:11–12; Ephesians 6:4*

Keywords: *Communication; Fathers; Foolishness; Immaturity; Impatience; Men; Parenting; Respect; Teenagers; Wisdom; Youth*

The classic 1955 film *Rebel Without a Cause* is the timeless story of the inner conflict of youth and the search for purpose and self-identity.

In one scene, Jim (played by James Dean) is lying on his bed fully clothed, with a sheet over his face. He has just been in a knife fight with another teenage boy.

Internally, Jim is struggling with his decision to join the other boy in a "chicken run" facing a cliff. They would speed toward the cliff in their cars, and the first to jump out is the chicken.

His father (played by Jim Backus) enters the room wearing a full-body apron over a business suit. He has been doing some cooking.

Jim asks his father, "Suppose you had to do something, you had to go someplace and do this thing that was—you knew it was very dangerous, but it was a matter of honor. And you had to prove it. What would you do?"

His father tries to dodge the question, asking if it required some kind of trick answer, and that Jim should never make a hasty decision. He turns on the light and sees bloodstains on Jim's white shirt. He asks, "What kind of trouble are you in?"

Jim answers, "The kind I was telling you about. Now can't you answer me?"

Once again the father tries to evade the question as he gets a towel from the adjacent bathroom. Jim gives a look of frustration and defeat. He takes off his shirt, and his father wipes a small nick of blood from his chest. Jim's dad says they should take time to look at all the alternatives and get some advice.

But Jim says he doesn't have time. Jim asks, "What can you do when you have to be a man?" His father hesitates, and Jim angrily demands, "No, you give me a direct answer!"

The dad tries to reason with Jim, "Listen, you're at a wonderful age. In ten years you'll look back on this and wish that . . ."

"Ten years?" Jim retorts. "I want an answer now!"

The father says, "Listen, Jimbo, I'm just trying to show you how foolish you are. When you're older, you'll look back on this and you'll laugh at yourself for thinking this is so important."

Jim grabs a jacket and walks out of the room. He flings his jacket around in frustration. As his father calls for him at the front door, Jim goes through the kitchen door and drives off.

Elapsed time: This scene begins at 00:41:50 and ends at 00:45:02.

Content: Not rated

Citation: *Rebel Without a Cause* (Warner Brothers, 1955), written by Stewart Stern (based on Irving Shulman's adaptation of "The Blind Run," a story by Dr. Robert M. Lindner), directed by Nicholas Ray

submitted by Jerry De Luca,
Montreal West, Quebec, Canada

93. TEMPTATION

Quiz Show

Topic: *Snare of Temptation*

Texts: *Ecclesiastes 5:10; Matthew 6:13;*
Mark 1:12–13; Luke 4:1–13; Luke 12:15;
Acts 24:16; 1 Corinthians 7:5;
1 Thessalonians 3:5; 1 Timothy 6:9–10;
2 Timothy 3:2; 1 Peter 3:16

Keywords: *Character; Choices; Conscience; Decisions;*
Fame; Greed; Media; Money; Resisting Temptation;
Temptation

Robert Redford's 1994 film *Quiz Show* is based on the television game show scandals of the mid 1950s. Brainy but not flashy, Herbert Stempel (played by John Turturro) was winning at NBC's "Twenty-One" for several weeks before the producers decided they wanted a more charismatic winning contestant to improve the ratings. They tried to convince young and handsome Professor Charles Van Doren (played by Ralph Fiennes) to secretly accept the questions and answers ahead of time so he could become the show's new star. They also tried to convince Stempel to intentionally lose on a question, for which they would reward him later. Stempel couldn't decide what to do, while Van Doren told the producers he wouldn't cheat.

At the start of the scene, Stempel and Van Doren are both in their soundproof booths. The host asks Stempel the question he was requested to get wrong: "Which movie won the Academy Award for Best Picture in 1955?" Stempel looks at the producers and pauses.

Backstage and at home, people are uttering the answer—*Marty*—indicating the question's simplicity. Sweat drips from his head as he deliberates whether to answer honestly or to lie. The host asks him if he wants to take a guess. Finally Stempel answers, "Best Picture: *On the Waterfront*." The host says, "Sorry, the answer is *Marty*."

Then the host turns to Van Doren: "The category is Civil War." Van Doren selects the eleven-point question, which would make him the new champion if he answers correctly. The host asks him a question on which he has been coached. Van Doren's face goes blank as he hears the familiar question. He is momentarily stunned. He says to himself, "It's just so oddly familiar." He takes his time as he struggles between right and wrong. Finally he gives the answer: "Yes, I know the name. General H. W. Halleck." He repeats the answer he was given backstage and is declared the new champion.

Elapsed time: Measured from the beginning of the opening credit, this scene begins at 00:31:35 and ends at 00:35:22.

Content: Rated PG-13 for language and mature themes

Citation: *Quiz Show* (Hollywood Pictures, 1994), written by Paul Attanasio (based on the book *Remembering America: A Voice from the Sixties* by Richard N. Goodwin), directed by Robert Redford

submitted by Jerry De Luca,
Montreal West, Quebec, Canada

94. THANKFULNESS

Shenandoah

Topic: *Thanking God*

Texts: *Deuteronomy 8:1–18; Psalm 145:15–16; Proverbs 28:26; Jeremiah 17:5–8; Matthew 6:11; Matthew 6:25–34; Luke 12:22–34; Romans 1:21; Romans 11:36*

Keywords: *Believing Prayer; Brokenness; Daily Bread; Dependence on God; Difficulties; God's Providence; God's Works; Gratitude; Hardship; Humility; Independent Spirit; Prayer; Pride; Provision; Self-Reliance; Self-Sufficiency; Thankfulness; Thanksgiving*

In the classic Western *Shenandoah,* James Stewart stars as Charlie Anderson, a Virginian farmer trying to keep his family out of the Civil War.

With a place setting laid out for his dead wife, and with his children gathered around the supper table, Charlie begins a litany they obviously have heard before: "Now your mother wanted all of you raised as good Christians, and I might not be able to do that thorny job as well as she could, but I can do a little something about your manners."

He gestures that they all should bow their heads and continues. "Lord, we cleared this land, we plowed it, sowed it, and harvested it. We cooked the harvest. We wouldn't be here, we wouldn't be eatin', if we hadn't done it all ourselves. We worked dog-boned hard for every crumb and morsel, but we thank you just the same anyway, Lord, for the food we're about to eat. Amen."

Through the course of the movie, we see one tragedy after another strike the Anderson clan: the youngest son is mistaken for a soldier and captured, another son and his wife are murdered by marauders, and a third son is shot by an overzealous sentry. When we next see Mr. Anderson at the supper table, there are four more empty places as he begins his ritual prayer. But this time we hear his voice quiver and break as the awful realization comes on him that he is not in control, that he is not the master of his own destiny. His voice trails off as he finishes the words "if we hadn't done it all ourselves."

He stops, gets up, and walks away, a proud man broken and stripped of his pride, knowing that he needs to turn to the Lord, but not yet ready to fall on his knees and ask for God's help.

Elapsed time: Measured from the beginning of the opening credit, the first prayer scene starts at 00:04:51 and ends at 00:05:22; the second prayer scene starts at 01:38:24 and ends at 01:39:15.

Content: Rated PG

Citation: *Shenandoah* (Universal Pictures, 1965), written by James Lee Barrett, directed by Andrew V. McLaglen

submitted by Alan Beck,
Souris, Prince Edward Island, Canada

95. TRANSFORMATION

Pygmalion

Topic: *Changed by Mercy*

Texts: *Romans 2:4; Colossians 3:12–14; Titus 3:3–5; 2 Peter 3:9*

Keywords: *Affirmation; Discipleship; Edification; Encouragement; Gentleness; God's Goodness; God's Love; Human Worth; Kindness; Mentoring; New Heart; New Life; Self-Image; Self-Worth; Spiritual Formation; Transformation; Words; Worth*

George Bernard Shaw gave an ancient Greek legend a twentieth-century twist when he retold the story of Pygmalion. In the legend, Pygmalion creates a wonderful statue of a maiden and begs the gods to give the statue life, which they do. (The 1964 Warner Brothers classic musical *My Fair Lady* is another version of the same story.)

Shaw's silver screen adaptation features a professor, Henry Higgins—the world's leading authority on speech and diction (played by Leslie Howard). He prides himself on being able to identify any Londoner's residence within a few blocks just by listening to his or her dialect. The professor's friend Colonel Pickering (played by Scott Sunderland) bets Higgins that he can't take a Cockney flower girl and pass her off as a lady after just three months of instruction. This challenge is too much to resist for the haughty Higgins, and he chooses Eliza Doolittle (played by Wendy Hiller) as the object of his experiment.

With drills, lessons, and insensitive threats, Higgins drives Eliza like a slave master. At one point Higgins says, "Eliza, you're an idiot. I waste the treasures of my Miltonic mind [on you]." Pickering tries to soften the professor's treatment of Eliza, but to him she is nothing but a laboratory experiment.

The great day arrives, and Higgins unveils his "experiment" at a royal reception. Eliza enters wearing jewels and a gown. She walks gracefully, demonstrates impeccable manners, and dances divinely. Her diction is pure, her conversation refined. No one dreams that Eliza is a "guttersnipe," and she becomes the toast of London. Higgins later touts his own genius: "I created this thing out of squashed cabbage leaves."

After the reception, as Higgins and Pickering unwind in the study, they hardly notice Eliza. Finally she confronts the mighty professor: Yes, he may have changed her dialect, but the kindness of Colonel Pickering changed her heart. He is the real Pygmalion. His gentle affirmation through the months of criticism and toil made the difference.

Eliza then says to Colonel Pickering, "I owe so much to you. . . . It was from you that I learned really nice manners, and that's what makes one a lady, isn't it?"

Pickering bashfully responds, "No doubt. Still he taught you to speak, you know, and I couldn't have done that."

"Of course," says Eliza. "That was his profession. It's just like learning to dance in the fashionable way, nothing more than that in it. You know what began my real education? Your calling me 'Miss Doolittle' that day when I first came to [the professor's study]. That was the beginning of self-respect for me. You see, the difference between a lady and a flower girl isn't how she behaves. It's how she is treated. I know that I shall always be a flower girl to Professor Higgins because he always treats me as a flower girl and always will. But I know that I can be a lady to you because you always treat me as a lady and always will."

Elapsed time: Measured from the beginning of the opening credit, this scene begins at 01:20:00 and ends at 01:22:40.

Content: Not rated

Citation: *Pygmalion* (MGM, 1938), written by Ian Dalrymple, Cecil Lewis, W. P. Lipscomb, and George Bernard Shaw (based on the play by George Bernard Shaw), directed by Anthony Asquith and Leslie Howard

submitted by Jeff Arthurs, South Hamilton, Massachusetts

96. TRANSFORMATION

A Walk to Remember

Topic: *When Someone Believes in You*

Texts: *1 Corinthians 13:7–8; Philippians 4:13; 1 Timothy 1:12–16*

Keywords: *Calling; Change; Example; Growth; Hope; Love; Ministry; Redemption; Relationships; Sanctification; Spiritual Formation; Transformation; Trust*

A *Walk to Remember,* based on the novel by Nicholas Sparks, illustrates how one person's life and death can have a positive impact on an entire community. Jamie Sullivan (played by Mandy Moore) is the high school daughter of a widowed minister in a small North Carolina town. The party crowd at the local high school scoffs at her conservative appearance and values. Yet Jamie remains resolute in her determination to be her own person.

When Jamie befriends Landon Carter (played by Shane West), one of those who's been mocking her, her father and Landon's friends are understandably concerned. But Jamie (who is dying of leukemia) quietly proves how unconditional love can have a transforming impact.

Landon has been up all night with Jamie, watching stars through a telescope at the local cemetery. Early in the morning, as he returns home, he encounters his mom (played by Daryl Hannah) on the back deck. Aware of the less-than-pure interaction Landon has had with previous girlfriends, his mother cautions him to be careful with "the minister's daughter." Landon assures her that their relationship is different.

His mother then pulls a folded sheet of paper from a folder on the patio table. "I was doing laundry the other day, and I found this," she says, unfolding the notebook paper.

Landon, obviously embarrassed, looks away. She has discovered a list of life goals he has written.

His mother reads aloud the words on the paper: "Examine a moon rock. Go to college. Get into medical school." She then adds, "Honey, these are beautiful ambitions. They're . . ." She starts to say how unrealistic they are for someone like him, but she catches herself and simply adds, "You're going to have to work really hard."

"I can do that!" Landon insists. He looks to the ground and begins to smile. "Mom," he says, "Jamie has faith in me. You know? She makes me want to be different—better!"

Elapsed time: This scene begins at 01:07:00 and ends at about 01:09:00.

Content: Rated PG for mild profanity and some sensual elements

Citation: *A Walk to Remember* (Warner Brothers, 2002), written by Karen Janszen (based on the novel by Nicholas Sparks), directed by Adam Shankman

submitted by Greg Asimakoupoulos, Naperville, Illinois

97. TRUST

Titanic

Topic: *Invitation to Trust*

Texts: *Psalm 22:4; Matthew 14:25–33; Luke 19:9–10; John 14:1*

Keywords: *Accepting Christ; Born Again; Conversion; Freedom; New Life; Risk; Trust*

The blockbuster *Titanic* tells the tale of how, on that ill-fated voyage, Jack Dawson (played by Leonardo DiCaprio) won the affection of a wealthy young woman named Rose Bukater (played by Kate Winslet).

Although Rose turns Jack away at first, she yearns for someone to break her free of her dismal life. She says, "Outwardly I was everything a well-brought-up girl should be. Inside I was screaming. I felt like I was standing at a great precipice, with no one to pull me back, no one who cared—or even noticed."

In perhaps the most famous scene of the movie, Rose has decided to give their romance a chance and has sought out Jack on the bow of the ship. When he sees her change of heart toward him, he reaches out to her and says, "Take my hand." He asks her not to speak but to close her eyes, and then he leads her to the very bow of the ship. He has her stand up on the railing, while he holds her steady. He asks Rose, "Do you trust me?"

She responds, "I trust you."

The scene radiates as the sunset streaks in the background. As Jack stretches out her arms over the bow and tells her to open her eyes, she's overwhelmed by the beauty of the water and the sunset before her. All she can say is, "I'm flying!"

Rose is being rescued from a predictable and passionless life and invited to pursue something more. This is what happens in our new life in Jesus Christ. Jesus extends himself to us and commands graciously, "Take my hand." Then he asks one simple question: "Do you trust me?" What follows is pure adventure.

Elapsed time: Measured from the beginning of the opening credit, this scene begins at 01:18:00 and lasts about two minutes.

Content: Rated PG-13 for nudity, violence, and profanity

Citation: *Titanic* (Paramount Pictures, 1997), written and directed by James Cameron

submitted by Bill White, Paramount, California

98. TRUTHFULNESS

The Man in the Gray Flannel Suit

Topic: *Integrity Checked*

Texts: *Psalm 25:21; Proverbs 13:6; Proverbs 30:7–9; Philippians 4:8; Colossians 3:9–10*

Keywords: *Business; Career; Character; Conduct; Honesty; Integrity; Lying; Morals; Responsibility; Success; Truthfulness; Work*

The 1956 film *The Man in the Gray Flannel Suit* stars Gregory Peck as Thomas Rath, a husband with three children. Thomas makes a meager $7,000 a year, with which he is satisfied. His wife, Betsy (played by Jennifer Jones), knows that since the war (World War II) Thomas hasn't been the go-getter he once was. She demands to know what happened to him, lambasting him for his lack of optimism.

At his wife's urging, Thomas seeks employment with the United Broadcasting Corporation. After getting the job, Thomas finds himself involved in the pet project of Ralph Hopkins, the president of UBC—a national campaign on mental health. Hopkins (played by Fredric March), is scheduled to give a speech before a large group of mental health professionals. So crucial is the speech he asks Thomas to critique it. To Thomas, the speech is "dreadful," yet he's reluctant to tell his boss the truth, fearful of the ramifications. In this scene, Betsy pleads for Thomas to be honest.

Thomas explains to Betsy, "I've told you that this is a loaded situation with all kinds of angles to it. But there's another side to it, which I think you must have overlooked. It just so happens that I have landed in one of the neatest positions in the whole organization, right next to Hopkins himself. It's a spot that three-quarters of the people at UBC would give their right arms for, and he likes me—I know it. Now will you try to remember what that could mean to us if I handle it carefully?"

Betsy adds, "If you handle it carefully and honestly, yes."

Thomas questions, "Aren't you the one who wanted more money, a new house, no more worries every week?"

"I still do." Betsy admits, "But that wasn't the real idea. The real idea was that I wanted you to go out and fight for something again, like the fellow I married. Not to turn into a cheap, slippery 'yes' man."

Thomas says, "That's wonderful. But would you think about this for a minute or two? When a man's got plenty of security, money in the bank, other jobs waiting for him, it's a cinch to be fearless and full of integrity. But when he's got a wife and three children to support, and his job's all he's got, what do you think he ought to do about it then?"

"I know what I'd do," Betsy states firmly.

Thomas laments, "I never wanted to get into this rat race, but now that I'm in it I think I'd be an idiot not to play it the way everybody else plays it."

Betsy responds, "For a decent man there's never any peace of mind without honesty, and I've always thought of you as a decent man. Right now it just makes me wonder how long it'll be before you decide it'll be simpler and safer not to tell me the truth."

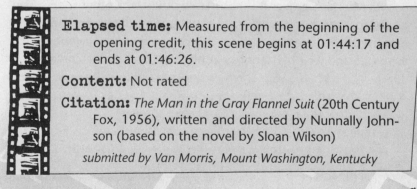

Elapsed time: Measured from the beginning of the opening credit, this scene begins at 01:44:17 and ends at 01:46:26.

Content: Not rated

Citation: *The Man in the Gray Flannel Suit* (20th Century Fox, 1956), written and directed by Nunnally Johnson (based on the novel by Sloan Wilson)

submitted by Van Morris, Mount Washington, Kentucky

99. UNBELIEF

12 Angry Men

Topic: Willingness to Consider the Truth of the Gospel

Texts: Mark 8:11–13; Acts 1:3; Acts 17:17–32; Romans 1:18–32; Romans 2:1–8

Keywords: Belief; Doubt; Evidence of God; Gospel; Prejudice; Proof; Salvation and Lostness; Skepticism

In the 1957 movie *12 Angry Men,* a young man's fate is in the hands of twelve jurists. He is on trial for the murder of his father.

The twelve jurists walk into a hot, cramped jury room. All but one of the jurists (played by Henry Fonda) are ready to be done with the inconvenience of this trial. They've heard all they want to hear and seem unwilling to consider the possibility that the young man could be innocent. Only Henry Fonda's character (Mr. Davis) seems sensitive to the fact that something important hangs in the balance—a man's life.

As Mr. Davis argues for reasonable doubt, the others don't want to listen. One man points to the unique murder weapon as proof positive of the defendant's guilt. Everyone seems convinced the knife is so rare and the boy's story so implausible that the defendant must be guilty. Frustrated with Davis as the lone holdout, he says, "Take a look at that knife. It's a very unusual knife. I've never seen one like it." The other men in the room murmur agreement.

"I'm just saying it's possible," says Davis.

One of the jurists steps forward angrily and shouts, "It's not possible!"

At that moment, Davis reaches calmly into his pocket, pulls out an identical knife, pops the blade, and plants it into the middle of the table.

"Where did you get that?" one jurist asks.

Davis responds, "I went out walking for a couple of hours last night. I walked through the boy's neighborhood. I bought that at a little pawn shop just two blocks from the boy's house. It cost six dollars."

Mr. Davis alone stopped long enough to take an honest, careful, unbiased look at the evidence. His courageous confrontation with the evidence ultimately reveals an astonishing truth: the defendant is innocent. One by one, through honest struggle, all the jurists come to the same conclusion, and a young man facing death is set free.

Likewise, considering the gospel requires putting prejudices aside and contemplating the evidence carefully, because something important hangs in the balance—a person's life.

Elapsed time: This scene begins at 00:26:48 and ends at 00:27:50.

Content: Not rated (little objectionable content)

Citation: *12 Angry Men* (United Artists, 1957), written by Reginald Rose (based on his television play), directed by Sidney Lumet

submitted by David Slagle, Wilmore, Kentucky

100. VENGEANCE

Dead Man Walking

Topic: *Vengeance and Mercy*

Texts: *Luke 6:37; Romans 5:6–10; Romans 12:19–21*

Keywords: *Anger; Bitterness; Conflict; Hatred; Human Worth; Justice; Mercy; Ministry; Murder; Vengeance*

Dead Man Walking is based on a true story about Sister Helen Prejean (played by Susan Sarandon), a nun who agrees to offer spiritual counsel to Matthew Poncelet (played by Sean Penn), a man on death row. This angers Mr. and Mrs. Percy, the parents of the teenage girl Poncelet murdered, as they can't understand how she could sympathize with someone who committed such a savage act.

In one scene, Sister Helen is sitting down with Mr. and Mrs. Percy (played by R. Lee Ermey and Celia Weston) in their home. Mrs. Percy asks her why she had come over to "our side." Sister Helen, with a concerned look on her face, carefully answers, "I wanted to come and see if I could help you all and pray with you, but he asked me to be his spiritual adviser, to be with him when he dies."

Mrs. Percy asks her what she said. Sister Helen answers, "That I would."

Mr. Percy has a surprised look on his face. "We thought that you changed your mind. We thought that's why you were here." Sister Helen shakes her head reluctantly.

Mrs. Percy, indignant, says, "How can you come here?" Mr. Percy says, "How can you sit with that scum?"

Sister Helen, somewhat anxious and groping for words, answers, "Mr. Percy, I've never done this before. I'm just trying to follow the example of Jesus, who said that every person is worth more than their worst act."

Mr. Percy responds in a passionate tone, "This is not a person. This is an animal. No, I take that back. Animals don't rape and murder their own kind. Matthew Poncelet is God's mistake. And you want to hold the poor murderer's hand. You want to be there to comfort him when he dies. There wasn't anybody in the woods that night to comfort Hope when those two animals pushed her face down into the wet grass!"

Sister Helen, in a flustered voice, says, "I just want to help him to take responsibility for what he did."

The parents respond with further indignation. Then Mr. Percy says in a firm, serious tone, "Sister, I think you need to leave this house right now." Sister Helen, now confused and flustered, stands up and heads toward the door. Mr. Percy stands and tells her angrily, "Wait a minute. If you really are sorry, and you really do care about this family, you want to see justice done for our murdered child. Now, you can't have it both ways. You can't befriend that murderer and expect to be our friend, too!"

Mrs. Percy adds, "You've brought the enemy into our house, Sister. You've got to go."

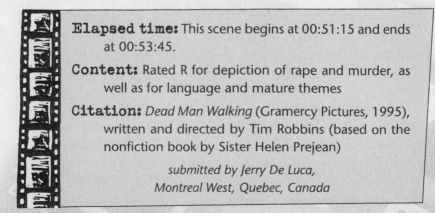

Elapsed time: This scene begins at 00:51:15 and ends at 00:53:45.

Content: Rated R for depiction of rape and murder, as well as for language and mature themes

Citation: *Dead Man Walking* (Gramercy Pictures, 1995), written and directed by Tim Robbins (based on the nonfiction book by Sister Helen Prejean)

submitted by Jerry De Luca,
Montreal West, Quebec, Canada

101. VISION

Lawrence of Arabia

Topic: *Importance of Vision*

Texts: *Genesis 15:1–2; Hosea 12:9–10; Zechariah 1:8; Acts 9:10–12*

Keywords: *Ambition; Calling; Convictions; Courage; Determination; Human Will; Inspiration of Persons; Leadership; Miracles; Mission; Motivation; Planning; Prayer; Vision*

Lawrence of Arabia is based on the true-life adventures of T. E. Lawrence (played by Peter O'Toole), a British military officer who was passionate about the people and land of the Middle East. During World War I he courageously united several enemy Arab tribes into a powerful guerrilla army to fight the ruling Turkish Empire.

In the movie, an Arab leader tells Lawrence that if the Arabs are to be free from the Turks and to be great again, they need a miracle. Contemplating how to defeat the Turks, Lawrence traverses the desert on a windy evening. His young assistants observe from a distance.

Night turns to morning, and Lawrence sits at the bottom of a small hill with his head down. His two assistants are at the top of the hill watching him. One of them intentionally drops a rock and lets it slide along the sand toward Lawrence's back. Lawrence reaches behind him, takes the rock, and oblivious to the bystanders, stands up and walks away.

Later during the day, Lawrence sits with his two assistants. They stare at Lawrence's focused face. His right hand shakes for a moment. Then he raises his head slightly and calmly says, "Aqaba. Aqaba. From the land."

The scene quickly shifts to a meeting between an Arab leader, Sherif Ali ibn el Kharish (played by Omar Sharif), and Lawrence. Sherif Ali is astounded by Lawrence's plan to defeat the Turks. He says, "You are mad! To come to Aqaba by land you should have to cross the Nefu Desert. The Nefu cannot be crossed. It takes more than a compass, Englishman. The Nefu is the worst place God created."

Lawrence replies, "I can't answer for the place—only for myself. Fifty men."

They continue to argue, but Lawrence assures Sherif Ali that other Arabs who live near Aqaba will join them and that the Turkish guns face the sea, not the desert. Lawrence leads him out of the tent and points forward. "Aqaba is over there. It's only a matter of going."

Sherif Ali turns around and tells him, "You are mad."

Ultimately, they make a seemingly impossible journey through a scorching desert, get help from other Arabs near Aqaba, take Aqaba by surprise, and win a decisive victory in the battle against the Turks.

Elapsed time: Measured from the beginning of the opening credit, this scene begins at 00:48:05 and ends at 00:52:06.

Content: Rated PG for violence and mature themes

Citation: *Lawrence of Arabia* (Columbia Pictures, 1962), written by Robert Bolt (based on *The Seven Pillars of Wisdom* by T. E. Lawrence), directed by David Lean

submitted by Jerry De Luca,
Montreal West, Quebec, Canada

Movie Title Index

Scripture Index

Romans

1 Corinthians

Keywords Index

Notes

Notes

Notes

Preaching That Connects
Using Journalistic Techniques to Add Impact

Mark Galli and Craig Brian Larson

Like everyone else, preachers long to be understood. Unfortunately, the rules first learned in seminary, if misapplied, can quickly turn homiletic precision into listener boredom.

To capture the heart and mind, Mark Galli and Craig Larson suggest that preachers turn to the lessons of journalism. In *Preaching That Connects*, they show how the same keys used to create effective, captivating communication in the media can transform a sermon.

Amply illustrated from some of today's best preachers, *Preaching That Connects* walks through the entire sermon, from the critical introduction to the bridge to illustrations and final application. Key points include the five techniques for generating creative ideas, your six options for illustrations, and the ten rules for great storytelling—and why the transition sentence is the hardest sentence you'll write.

Preaching That Connects is for all who seek to hone their craft so they can communicate the truth of the gospel effectively.

Softcover: 0-310-38621-7

Pick up a copy today at your favorite bookstore!

ZONDERVAN™

GRAND RAPIDS, MICHIGAN 49530 USA

WWW.ZONDERVAN.COM

Movie-Based Illustrations for Preaching and Teaching
101 Clips to Show or Tell

Craig Brian Larson
and Andrew Zahn

Movies have become the stories of our culture. People love to discuss favorite movies and actors, and this interest can help you communicate God's Word with power—if you have exciting, movie-based illustrations at your fingertips.

This collection contains 101 complete illustrations straight from popular movies your listeners can relate to—*The Matrix*, *Beauty and the Beast*, *It's a Wonderful Life*, *Chariots of Fire*, and many more.

- Complete index includes multiple keywords, relevant Scripture passages, and movie titles for easy selection.
- Each illustration provides plot summary and detailed description of the scene—you can tell the story well even if you haven't seen the movie.
- Exact begin and end times are given for each illustration if you wish to show the video clip.
- Each illustration gives background information on the movie—year created, MPAA rating, and more.

This handy, to-the-point resource will help you add dramatic muscle to your sermons and lessons. Engage your listeners' imaginations through the power of movies—and drive biblical truths home to their hearts.

Softcover: 0-310-24832-9

Pick up a copy today at your favorite bookstore!

A SPECIAL INVITATION...

...to participate with some of today's prominent pastors and communicators

Join them and over 23,000 members on one of today's premier online resources.

*P*reachingToday.com provides you with a powerful, searchable database to help you quickly find the right illustrations for your sermons. The database contains over 7,700 top-quality sermon illustrations selected by the editors of *Leadership*.

- **Prepare your sermons and preach with confidence** with the help of *Skill Builders*. Over 100 full sermon outlines, preaching tips and articles by senior editor **Haddon Robinson** and many of today's best communicators.

- **Preach fresh, timely sermons** with 10 NEW illustrations e-mailed to you every week. All are indexed by topic and Bible text, including the week's lectionary and NEW movie illustrations.

- **Get ideas and tips** when you link to other great preaching resources from *Leadership* journal, *Books & Culture*, *Christianity Today*, *Christian History*, and more...

As a benefit for purchasing this book, we would like to offer you a **FREE 90-DAY TRIAL** to *PreachingToday.com*.

To sign up, visit:

www.PreachingToday.com/go/moviebook

We want to hear from you. Please send your comments about this book to us in care of zreview@zondervan.com. Thank you.

ZONDERVAN™

GRAND RAPIDS, MICHIGAN 49530 USA

WWW.ZONDERVAN.COM